P · O · C · K · E · T · S

SCIENCE FACTS

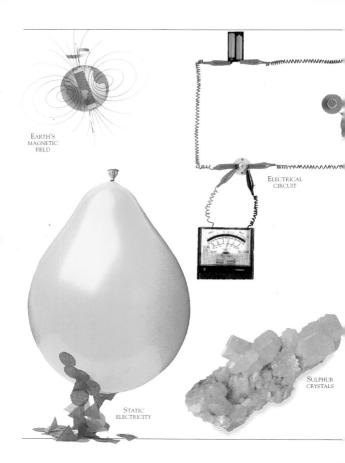

EARTH'S
MAGNETIC
FIELD

ELECTRICAL
CIRCUIT

STATIC
ELECTRICITY

SULPHUR
CRYSTALS

P · O · C · K · E · T · S

SCIENCE FACTS

Written by
STEVE SETFORD

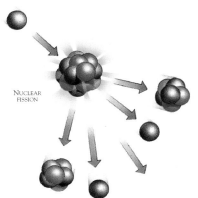

NUCLEAR
FISSION

TITRATION
TEST

DORLING KINDERSLEY
London • New York • Stuttgart

A DORLING KINDERSLEY BOOK

Project editor   Scarlett O'Hara
Designers   Jacqui Burton
Carlton Hibbert
Senior editor   Hazel Egerton
Senior art editor   Jacquie Gulliver
Editorial consultant   Jack Challoner
Picture research   Lorna Ainger
Production   Josie Alabaster

First published in Great Britain in 1996
by Dorling Kindersley Limited
9 Henrietta Street, Covent Garden, London WC2E 8PS

Reprinted 1996

A CIP catalogue record for this book is available from
the British Library

ISBN 0 7513 5368 X

Colour reproduction by Colourscan, Singapore
Printed and bound in Italy by L.E.G.O.

CONTENTS

HOW TO USE THIS BOOK

These pages show you how to use *Pockets: Science Facts*. The book is divided into eight sections. Each section contains information on a particular aspect of science. The pages in that section give further information on the subject including diagrams and charts. There is a glossary and index at the back of the book.

RUNNING HEADS
The running heads act as a reminder of the section of the book you are in. The left-hand running head indicates the section and the right-hand running head shows the subject of the page.

Running head

Corner coding

Heading

Introduction

ATOMS

MATTER IS MADE UP of tiny particles called atoms. Since most atoms are very stable structures, they form the building blocks for everything in the universe. There are just over a hundred types of atom, which are themselves made up of even smaller "subatomic" particles.

Electron shell

ATOMIC STRUCTURE
The centre, or nucleus, contains protons (which have positive charge) and neutrons (which have no charge). Negatively charged particles called electrons orbit the nucleus in layers,

CARBON-12 ATOM

Orbiting electron

Nucleus

NUCLEON NUMBER
The total number of protons and neutrons in the nucleus is the atom's nucleon number. The most common form of carbon has 6 protons and 6 neutrons, so it is called carbon-12.

Proton

CARBON-12 ATOM

ISOTOPES
All atoms of the same element have the same number of protons, but forms of the element may have different numbers of neutrons. These atoms are called isotopes. The isotope carbon-14 has two more neutrons than the isotope carbon-12.

Nucleus contains 6 protons and 8 neutrons.

Annotation

Caption

CORNER CODING
Coloured boxes in the corners of each page tell you which section of the book you are in.

- MATTER
- ELEMENTS
- CHEMICAL CHANGES
- FORCE AND ENERGY
- LIGHT
- SOUND
- MAGNETISM AND ELECTRICITY
- HISTORY OF SCIENCE

HEADING AND INTRODUCTION
The heading describes the subject of a page. If a subject continues over more than one page the same heading applies. The introduction gives an overview of the subject.

CAPTIONS
Each illustration, whether photograph, artwork, or diagram, is accompanied by an explanatory caption.

ANNOTATIONS
Illustrations have annotations in *italics*. The annotation points out the features of diagrams and illustrations, often using leader lines.

FACT BOXES

The yellow boxes on many pages contain at-a-glance information and interesting, additional details about the subject. The fact box on this page contains atom facts.

SCIENTIFIC LAWS AND PRINCIPLES BOXES

Pink boxes highlight scientific laws or principles that relate to the topic on the page. Equations or formulae may be written out or principles explained. This box explains terms associated with atoms.

FEATURE BOXES

The feature boxes that appear on many pages pick out particular aspects of the main topic. The box may contain more detailed information and diagrams or explain a process that is related to the main topic on the page.

*Scientific laws and
principles box*

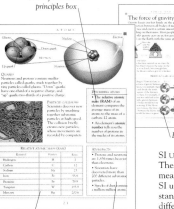

Feature box

SI units box

Chart

Fact box

CHARTS

Blue-coloured charts appear on many pages in the book. They supply facts and figures in an accessible way. This chart gives examples of relative atomic mass.

SI UNITS BOXES

These green boxes define the SI units of measurement appropriate to the topic. SI units are an international set of standard units that enable scientists in different countries to share information.

GLOSSARY AND INDEX

On the pale yellow pages at the back of the book, a glossary defines difficult words, and an index lists every subject alphabetically. By referring to the index, specific topics can be looked up easily.

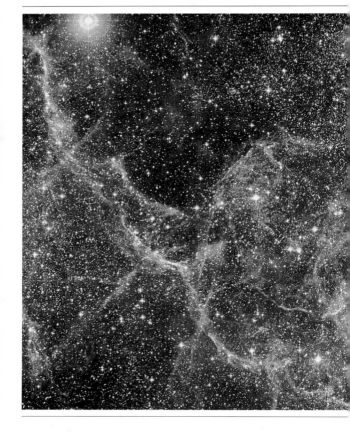

MATTER

WHAT IS MATTER?

MATTER IS all around us. Everything that exists in the universe is made up of matter – from the tiniest insect, to the distant stars in the night sky. Most matter is made up of minute particles called atoms. On Earth, matter usually occurs in one of three "states" (forms) called solid, liquid, or gas.

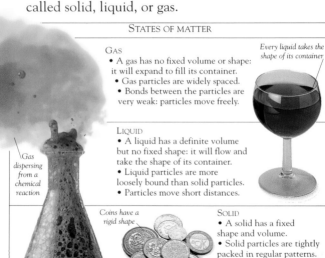

STATES OF MATTER

GAS
- A gas has no fixed volume or shape: it will expand to fill its container.
- Gas particles are widely spaced.
- Bonds between the particles are very weak: particles move freely.

Every liquid takes the shape of its container

Gas dispersing from a chemical reaction

LIQUID
- A liquid has a definite volume but no fixed shape: it will flow and take the shape of its container.
- Liquid particles are more loosely bound than solid particles.
- Particles move short distances.

Coins have a rigid shape

SOLID
- A solid has a fixed shape and volume.
- Solid particles are tightly packed in regular patterns.
- The particles can vibrate, though strong forces hold them firmly in place.

COMPARING MASS, DENSITY, AND VOLUME

MASS, DENSITY, AND VOLUME

Mass is the amount of matter in an object.
Volume is the space the object occupies.
An object's density is its mass divided
by its volume. Density is used to compare
the heaviness of different materials.

*Blocks of
equal mass but
unequal density*

WAX

BALSA

LEAD

*Density
11,300 kg/m³*

*Density
900 kg/m³*

*Density
200 kg/m³*

COMMON DENSITIES

The atoms of materials such as
metals have a greater mass and
are more tightly packed than the
atoms of materials such as wood.

MATERIAL	DENSITY KG/M³
Gold	19,300
Steel	7,900
Concrete	2,400
Water	1,000
Petrol	800
Wood (oak)	650
Air (at sea level)	1.025

PLASMA – THE FOURTH STATE OF MATTER

Plasma forms when electrons are torn
from their atoms by electricity or heat.
In this glass ball, plasma
forms when a strong
electric current
passes through
low-pressure gases.

Plasma streaks

Electrode

HYDROMETERS

A liquid's density is often
given relative to the density
of water. A hydrometer
measures the relative
density of liquids.
The level at which
the hydrometer
floats indicates
the density.

*Water's
relative
density
is 1*

*Cooking oil
has a relative
density of 0.91*

*Hydrometer
floats lower
in oil*

SI UNITS

The **kilogram** (kg) is the SI unit of mass.
It is equal to the mass of a block of
platinum alloy kept at Sèvres in France.
There are 1,000 milligrams (mg) in a
gram (g), 1,000 grams in a kilogram,
and 1,000 kilograms in a tonne (t).

Changing state

The state of a substance is determined by its temperature. When heated, solids change to liquids, and liquids to gases because their particles vibrate faster, weakening the bonds that hold the particles together. When cooled, gases change to liquids (condense), and liquids to solids. Their particles slow down and the bonds between them strengthen.

ICE

Ice forms when water is cooled sufficiently

Solid ice cubes have a definite shape and volume

THE THREE STATES OF WATER
When its temperature falls below 0°C (32°F), water takes the form of ice. If its temperature rises above 100°C (212°F), water turns to steam. Between these temperatures water is in its liquid state.

LIQUID WATER

When ice is heated it melts to form liquid water

Liquid water takes on the shape of the flask

Steam rises and escapes from the flask

STEAM

PRESSURE COOKING
The increased pressure inside a pressure cooker raises the boiling point of water because the water molecules need more heat energy to escape as a gas. The higher temperature cooks the food more quickly.

Safety valve lets out excess steam

Bubbles of steam form when the liquid is heated to boiling point

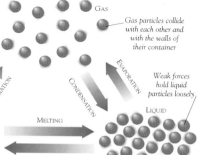

GAS CHANGES
• A gas condenses to a liquid.
• Condensation takes place at or below the boiling point.
• Sublimation occurs when a gas, such as carbon dioxide, changes to a solid without first forming a liquid.

Gas particles collide with each other and with the walls of their container

Weak forces hold liquid particles loosely

Solid particles are fixed rigidly in position

GAS

LIQUID

SOLID

SUBLIMATION

CONDENSATION

EVAPORATION

MELTING

FREEZING

SOLID CHANGES
• Above a temperature called the melting point, most solids become liquids.
• Many solids can change directly into a gas (sublime), without becoming a liquid first.

LIQUID CHANGES
• A liquid evaporates to form a gas. Above a temperature called its boiling point, all of the liquid becomes a gas.
• A liquid freezes to a solid below a temperature called its freezing point.

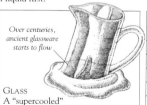

Over centuries, ancient glassware starts to flow

GLASS
A "supercooled" liquid such as glass can cool below its freezing point without solidifying. Glass is rigid, but its particles are arranged more randomly than those of a solid.

MELTING/FREEZING POINTS	
SUBSTANCE	MELTING POINT
Alcohol (ethanol)	–169°C (–272°F)
Water	0°C (32°F)
Wax	57°C (135°F)
PVC	197°C (387°F)
Nylon	212°C (414°F)
Salt (sodium chloride)	801°C (1,474°F)
Gold	1,064°C (1,947°F)
Steel (stainless)	1,527°C (2,781°F)
Diamond	3,550°C (6,422°F)

KINETIC THEORY

ACCORDING TO KINETIC THEORY, particles of matter are constantly in motion. The energy of the "kinetic" (moving) particles determines the temperature and behaviour of matter. The "gas laws" use kinetic theory to explain how gases behave.

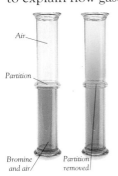

Air

Partition

Bromine and air

Partition removed

Diffusion of bromine gas in air

Particles of bromine and air are mixed evenly

DIFFUSION

The fast-moving particles of a gas spread out and occupy as much space as possible. This is why two gases quickly intermingle (diffuse) when they meet. Solids and liquids form solutions by diffusion, although they diffuse more slowly than gases.

MOVING MATTER FACTS

• Austrian physicist Ludwig Boltzmann developed kinetic theory in the 1860s.

• Scottish botanist Robert Brown observed Brownian motion in 1827. (Albert Einstein explained it in 1905.)

Pollen suspended in water

BROWNIAN MOTION

Seen under a microscope, pollen grains in water bounce about randomly. This phenomenon is called Brownian motion. It is caused by tiny, unseen water molecules that bombard the pollen grains.

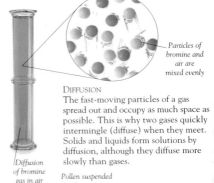

CHARLES' LAW IN ACTION

1 COOLING GAS
When a gas-filled balloon is placed in liquid nitrogen at −196°C (−321°F), the gas inside cools down.

Balloon collapses

2 SHRINKING VOLUME
Gas molecules slow down as the gas cools. The molecules collide less with the balloon walls, so the balloon shrinks.

Balloon expands

Liquid nitrogen

3 REFLATION
Removing the balloon from the liquid nitrogen lets the gas warm in the air. The gas molecules speed up and the balloon expands again.

EXPANSION RATES OF SELECTED MATERIALS

Heating a solid gives its atoms more kinetic energy. The atoms vibrate faster and take up more space, causing the solid to expand.

SUBSTANCE	EXPANSION OF HEATED 1 M BAR AT 100°C (212°F)
Invar (steel/nickel alloy)	0.1 mm
Pyrex	0.3 mm
Platinum alloy	0.9 mm
Steel	1.1 mm
Aluminium	2.6 mm

GAS LAWS

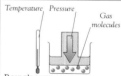

Temperature   Pressure

Gas molecules

BOYLE'S LAW
At constant temperature (T), the volume of a gas (V) is inversely proportional to the pressure (P) (the gas contracts if the pressure rises): PV=constant.

PRESSURE LAW
At constant volume, the pressure of a gas is proportional to the temperature (increasing the temperature raises the gas's pressure): P/T=constant.

CHARLES' LAW
At constant pressure, the volume of a gas is proportional to the temperature (the gas expands if the temperature rises): V/T=constant.

DESCRIBING MATTER

A MATERIAL CAN be described by its physical properties as well as by its chemical make-up. Colour, shape, texture, and smell are the simplest properties. Others include hardness, solubility, and viscosity, and the way a material behaves when forces act on it.

VISCOSITY
A viscous liquid such as honey does not flow easily because of friction between its molecules. Free-flowing liquids such as water have a low viscosity.

HONEYCOMB

The viscous honey spreads out very slowly

MOHS' SCALE OF HARDNESS		
HARDNESS	MINERAL	SCRATCHED BY
10	Diamond	Diamond only
9	Corundum	Silicon carbide
8	Topaz	Tungsten carbide
7	Quartz	Hard steel file
6	Feldspar	Sand
5	Apatite	Nickel
4	Fluorite	Glass
3	Calcite	Iron nail
2	Gypsum	Fingernail
1	Talc	Tin

HARDNESS
The ability to resist scratching is called hardness. It is measured on Mohs' scale, which compares the hardness of ten minerals. A material will scratch any other with a lower Mohs' rating.

DUCTILITY AND MALLEABILITY
Ductile solids such as copper can be stretched out into a wire. Malleable solids can be shaped while cold by hammering or rolling. Gold is the most malleable metal.

COPPER WIRE

ELASTICITY

RUBBER ATOMS

STRETCHED RUBBER

FURTHER STRETCHING

Strip is 15 cm long when no force acts upon it

1 kg mass stretches rubber to 17 cm

2 kg mass stretches rubber to 19 cm

1 ELASTICITY
Elastic solids such as this rubber strip get larger (extend) when stretched, get smaller when squeezed, and return to their normal size and shape when no force acts upon them.

2 STRETCHING
When a 1 kg mass is hung from the strip, the force of tension stretches the strip by 2 cm. The rubber atoms move apart as the bonds between them extend under tension.

3 DOUBLE STRETCHING
Doubling the force of tension will also double the stretching, so when a 2 kg mass is hung from the strip, the rubber stretches by 4 cm.

BRITTLENESS
Brittle materials break suddenly when stretched or squeezed, and shatter if given a sharp knock. But even fragile materials such as glass and pottery have some elasticity before they break.

Glass shatters into tiny pieces

A wine glass breaks easily if dropped on the floor

SOLUBILITY IN WATER

The following masses of each substance dissolve in 100 g of water at 25°C (77°F):

• Alcohol (ethanol): almost limitless

• Sugar: 211 g

• Salt: 36 g

• Carbon dioxide: 0.14 g

• Oxygen: 0.004 g

• Sand: insoluble

ATOMS

MATTER IS MADE UP of tiny particles called atoms. Since most atoms are very stable structures, they form the building blocks for everything in the universe. There are just over a hundred types of atom, which are themselves made up of even smaller "subatomic" particles.

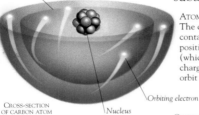

Electron shell

CROSS-SECTION
OF CARBON ATOM

Orbiting electron

Nucleus

ATOMIC STRUCTURE
The centre, or nucleus, of an atom contains protons (which have a positive charge) and neutrons (which have no charge). Negatively charged particles called electrons orbit the nucleus in layers, or "shells".

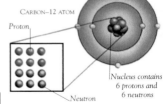

CARBON–12 ATOM

Proton

*Nucleus contains
6 protons and
6 neutrons*

Neutron

NUCLEON NUMBER
The total number of protons and neutrons in the nucleus is the atom's nucleon number. The most common form of carbon has 6 protons and 6 neutrons, so it is called carbon–12.

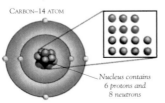

CARBON–14 ATOM

*Nucleus contains
6 protons and
8 neutrons*

ISOTOPES
All atoms of the same element contain the same number of protons, but some forms of the element may have different numbers of neutrons. These are isotopes. The isotope carbon–14 has two more neutrons than the isotope carbon–12.

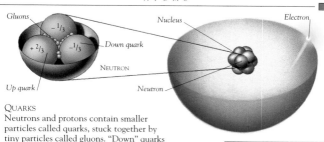

Gluons

Nucleus

Electron

$-\frac{1}{3}$ — Down quark

$+\frac{2}{3}$

$-\frac{1}{3}$

NEUTRON

Up quark

Neutron

QUARKS
Neutrons and protons contain smaller particles called quarks, stuck together by tiny particles called gluons. "Down" quarks have one-third of a negative charge, and "up" quarks two-thirds of a positive charge.

PARTICLE COLLISIONS
Scientists discover new particles by smashing together subatomic particles at high speed. The collision briefly creates new particles, whose movements are recorded by computers.

DESCRIBING ATOMS

• The **relative atomic mass (RAM)** of an element compares the average mass of its atoms to the mass of a carbon–12 atom.

• An element's **atomic number** tells you the number of protons in the nuclei of its atoms.

RELATIVE ATOMIC MASS (RAM)		
ELEMENT	SYMBOL	RAM
Hydrogen	H	1
Carbon	C	12
Sodium	Na	23
Iron	Fe	55.9
Bromine	Br	79.9
Tungsten	W	183.9
Mercury	Hg	200.6

ATOM FACTS

• Protons and neutrons are 1,836 times heavier than electrons.

• Scientists have discovered more than 200 different subatomic particles.

• Specks of dust contain a million million atoms.

RADIOACTIVITY

THE NUCLEI OF some atoms are radioactive. This means they are unstable and will decay (break up) over time. Most elements have unstable forms called radioisotopes. As they decay, they give out three types of radiation: alpha, beta, and gamma rays. Radiation can be very dangerous.

Alpha particle

Beta particle

Paper blocks alpha particles

Gamma ray

Aluminium blocks beta particles

RADIATION
Alpha rays are streams of positively charged particles made up of two neutrons and two protons. Beta rays are streams of electrons. Gamma rays, the most penetrating type of radiation, are electromagnetic waves.

Lead blocks gamma rays

SI UNITS:
The **becquerel** (Bq) is the unit of radioactivity. The radioactivity of a substance measured in becquerels is the number of its nuclei that decay each second.

Geiger counter

Dial shows amount of radioactivity

GEIGER COUNTER
When a radioactive particle enters a Geiger counter, it causes a brief pulse of electric current to flow. The radioactivity of a sample is calculated by the number of these pulses.

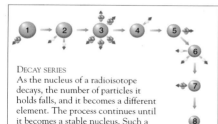

DECAY SERIES
As the nucleus of a radioisotope decays, the number of particles it holds falls, and it becomes a different element. The process continues until it becomes a stable nucleus. Such a sequence is called a decay series.

KEY TO DECAY SERIES
1. Alpha decay of uranium–238
2. Two stages of beta decay
3. Five stages of alpha decay
4. Beta decay of lead–214
5. Alpha decay of polonium–214
6. Three stages of beta decay
7. Alpha decay of polonium–210
8. The element lead–206 forms

RADIOACTIVE HALF-LIVES
The time taken for half of the nuclei in a radioactive substance to decay is called the substance's half-life. Over each half-life period, radioactivity falls first to a half, then to a quarter, and so on. The half-life of each radioisotope is different.

HALF-LIVES OF RADIOISOTOPES		
ISOTOPE	HALF-LIFE	TYPE OF DECAY
Uranium–238	4,500 million years	Alpha
Carbon–14	5,570 years	Beta
Cobalt–60	5.3 years	Gamma
Radon–222	4 days	Beta
Unnilquadium–105	32 seconds	Gamma

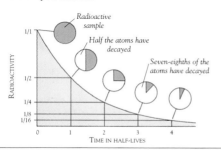

Radioactive sample

Half the atoms have decayed

Seven-eighths of the atoms have decayed

RADIOACTIVITY

1/1
1/2
1/4
1/8
1/16

0   1   2   3   4
TIME IN HALF-LIVES

RADIOACTIVITY FACTS
• Though radiation can be dangerous, it has many uses in medicine, including sterilizing equipment and killing cancer cells.

• Radioactivity was discovered by the French physicist Antoine Henri Becquerel in 1896.

BONDS AND MOLECULES

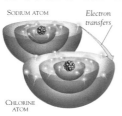

SODIUM ATOM

Electron transfers

CHLORINE ATOM

ATOMS MAY STICK together to form molecules by a process called "bonding". The bonds between atoms are electrical forces made by the movement of electrons. They form when atoms try to gain a full outer shell of electrons.

POSITIVELY CHARGED SODIUM ION

Both ions now have eight electrons in outer shell

Ionic bond

IONIC BONDS

In ionic bonding, electrons transfer between atoms, leaving the atoms as charged particles called ions. The atom losing the electron becomes a positive ion, or cation, and the atom gaining the electron becomes a negative ion, or anion. The force of attraction between the opposite charges forms a strong ionic bond.

NEGATIVELY CHARGED CHLORIDE ION

Positive sodium ion (Na^+)

Negative chloride ion (Cl^-)

SODIUM CHLORIDE

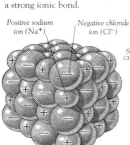

GIANT IONIC STRUCTURE

A crystal of salt (sodium chloride) contains sodium and chloride ions arranged in a regular network that extends throughout the crystal. This network is called a giant ionic lattice.

COVALENT BONDS

In covalent bonding, atoms share electrons. Two atoms each "donate" an electron, and the electrons form a pair that orbits both nuclei, holding the atoms together as a molecule. In a double bond, each atom donates two electrons.

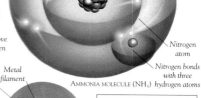

Hydrogen atom

Shared electrons form single bond

Nitrogen atom

Nitrogen bonds with three

AMMONIA MOLECULE (NH₃) *hydrogen atoms*

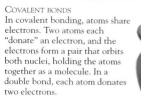

Electrons move freely between atoms

Metal filament

METALLIC BONDS

Electrons in the outer shell of metal atoms are loosely attached. These free-moving electrons form a common pool that bonds the atoms firmly together. They also make metals good conductors of heat and electricity.

LIGHT BULB

MOLECULE FACTS

• In 1811, the Italian Amedeo Avogadro was the first to distinguish molecules from atoms.

• At normal pressure and temperature, one litre of any gas contains 25,000 million million million molecules.

PARTICLES AND THEIR STRUCTURE FORMS			
STRUCTURE	COMPOSITION	TYPE OF SUBSTANCE	EXAMPLES
Metallic	Atoms	Metals	Sodium, iron, copper
Ionic	Ions	Compound of a metal with a non-metal	Sodium chloride (salt), calcium hydroxide (lime)
Simple molecular	Small molecules	Non-metal, or a non-metal compound	Iodine, sulphur, water, carbon dioxide
Giant molecular	Large molecules	Non-metal, or a non-metal compound	Diamond, graphite, polythene, sand

CRYSTALS

MOST SOLIDS have a crystalline structure, in which particles link up in regular, repeating patterns. There are seven basic crystal shapes, or crystal systems. All have straight edges, symmetrical corners, and smooth faces. Well-formed crystals are often prized for their beauty.

CRYSTAL FORMATION
• Crystals may form as a molten solid cools, or as a liquid evaporates from a solution.
• Atoms, ions, or molecules link up to form a framework called a lattice.
• The smallest complete piece of a lattice is a basic arrangement of particles called a unit cell.
• The lattice is made up of identical unit cells repeated many times over.

Sulphur forms both orthorhombic and monoclinic crystals

SULPHUR CRYSTALS

CRYSTAL FACTS

• Photographic film records images using special light-sensitive crystals of silver salts.

• Crystals of pure silicon are used in electronics. They are created artificially because they do not occur naturally.

• Diamonds are crystals of pure carbon.

This calculator displays figures using an LCD

LIQUID CRYSTALS
A liquid crystal can flow, but its particles line up in regular patterns. Heat or electricity can alter the pattern of the particles, and change the passage of light through the crystal. This process forms letters or numbers on a liquid-crystal display (LCD).

CRYSTAL SYSTEMS

Crystal systems are
based on the lengths
of any three edges
in the unit cell that
meet at a corner,
and the angles at
which they meet.

CUBIC CRYSTALS OF
GALENA (IRON ORE)

CUBIC SYSTEM
Every angle is 90°. All three
edges are equal in length.

TETRAGONAL SYSTEM
Every angle is 90°. Two of the
three edges are equal in length.

ORTHORHOMBIC SYSTEM
Every angle is 90°. None of the
three edges are of equal length.

MONOCLINIC SYSTEM
Two of the three edges meet at
90°. None are equal in length.

HEXAGONAL SYSTEM
Edges form angles of 90° and
120°. Two are of equal length.

TRIGONAL SYSTEM
None of the three edges meet
at 90°. All are of equal length.

TRICLINIC SYSTEM
None of the edges meet at 90°.
None are equal in length.

PIEZOELECTRIC CRYSTALS
Some crystals produce an electric
current when squeezed or made to
vibrate. When an electric current
is applied to them, they vibrate at
a precise frequency. They are used
in electronic devices and clocks.

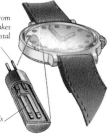

Current from
battery makes
quartz crystal
vibrate

Vibrating
crystal
controls
watch hands

WATER OF CRYSTALLIZATION
Some crystals are "hydrates",
meaning that they have water
molecules trapped inside them.
Heating blue copper sulphate
crystals drives off this "water of
crystallization", leaving white
"anhydrous" crystals behind.

Adding water
turns the
white crystals
blue again

MIXTURES AND COMPOUNDS

IN THE NATURAL WORLD, few elements exist alone.
Most substances are made up of two or more elements,
either mingled loosely as mixtures
or, after chemical reactions,
combined strongly as compounds.
The main types of mixtures
are solutions and colloids.

Potassium permanganate forms a solution in water

Water molecule attracts positively charged potassium ion

SOLUTIONS

A solution is a mixture of one
substance (the solute) dissolved
in another (the solvent). Many
compounds break down in water
into charged particles (ions) that
form weak bonds with water molecules.

COLLOIDS

In a colloid, tiny particles of
matter are dispersed evenly
throughout a solid,
liquid, or gas.
Hair gel is a
colloid of
solid fat
particles
that are
suspended
in water.

HAIR GEL

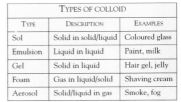

TYPES OF COLLOID		
TYPE	DESCRIPTION	EXAMPLES
Sol	Solid in solid/liquid	Coloured glass
Emulsion	Liquid in liquid	Paint, milk
Gel	Solid in liquid	Hair gel, jelly
Foam	Gas in liquid/solid	Shaving cream
Aerosol	Solid/liquid in gas	Smoke, fog

COMPARING MIXTURES AND COMPOUNDS
- A loose combination of sulphur and iron filings is a mixture. Heating the mixture causes a chemical reaction and forms a compound.
- The mixture separates easily with a magnet; the compound requires a chemical reaction.

Iron filings are attracted to a magnet

COMPOUND OF IRON SULPHIDE

Magnet does not attract new compound

MIXTURE OF IRON FILINGS AND SULPHUR

DIFFERENT COMPOUNDS

Copper and oxygen can form two different compounds. Copper(I) oxide contains twice as many copper atoms as oxygen atoms. Copper(II) oxide contains equal numbers of oxygen and copper atoms.

COPPER(I) OXIDE (Cu_2O)

COPPER(II) OXIDE (CuO)

PROPERTIES OF COMPOUNDS

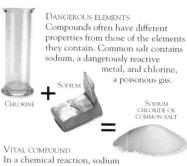

CHLORINE

SODIUM

SODIUM CHLORIDE OR COMMON SALT

DANGEROUS ELEMENTS
Compounds often have different properties from those of the elements they contain. Common salt contains sodium, a dangerously reactive metal, and chlorine, a poisonous gas.

VITAL COMPOUND
In a chemical reaction, sodium and chlorine combine to form white crystals of salt – the compound sodium chloride. The sodium and chlorine lose their dangerous properties. The resulting compound is not only safe and edible, but also a vital part of our diet.

Separating mixtures

Scientists need to separate mixtures in order to investigate
their components. Decanting involves pouring a liquid
off from a solid sediment or a denser liquid. Centrifuging
separates dense components from less dense ones by
spinning them round. Other separation methods include
distillation, evaporation, filtration, and desiccation.

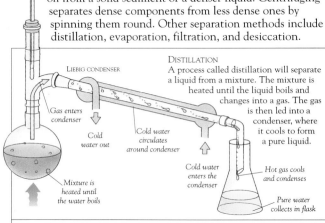

LIEBIG CONDENSER

*Gas enters
condenser*

*Cold
water out*

*Cold water
circulates
around condenser*

*Cold water
enters the
condenser*

*Mixture is
heated until
the water boils*

DISTILLATION

A process called distillation will separate
a liquid from a mixture. The mixture is
heated until the liquid boils and
changes into a gas. The gas
is then led into a
condenser, where
it cools to form
a pure liquid.

*Hot gas cools
and condenses*

*Pure water
collects in flask*

FRACTIONAL DISTILLATION

This process is used to
separate a mixture of liquids
with different boiling points.
To extract gases from air
for industrial use, the air
must be cooled first and
liquefied. As the air warms,
liquid gases boil off at
different temperatures.

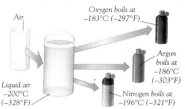

Air

Oxygen boils at
−183°C (−297°F)

Argon
boils at
−186°C
(−303°F)

*Liquid air
−200°C
(−328°F)*

Nitrogen boils at
−196°C (−321°F)

EVAPORATION

Heat can drive off a liquid from a mixture by making it evaporate. In tropical climates, evaporation is often used to obtain salt (sodium chloride) from sea water. Shallow salt pans, dug out on the coast, flood with sea water. The water evaporates in the sun, leaving salt crystals.

Filter paper holds back sulphur particles

FILTRATION

It is possible to separate large solid particles from a liquid mixture using a filter. A filter is a porous barrier that allows the liquid (the filtrate) to pass through, but holds back the solid particles (the residue).

Mixture of powdered sulphur and copper sulphate solution

Copper sulphate solution passes through filter paper

Airtight glass lid

Prism of rock salt to be kept dry

Silica gel desiccant absorbs moisture

DESICCATION

A desiccator removes water from a solid mixture. It is a sealed glass dish containing a moisture-absorbing substance called a desiccant. Rock salt is stored in a desiccator to keep it dry for laboratory use.

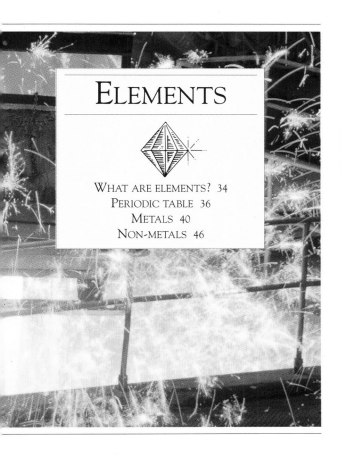

ELEMENTS

WHAT ARE ELEMENTS?

AN ELEMENT IS a substance made of only one type of atom. Of the 109 known elements, 89 occur naturally on Earth. The rest are made artificially. A few "unreactive" elements, such as gold, occur in their pure state; most form compounds with other elements.

VEINS OF PURE GOLD IN QUARTZ

ALLOTROPES OF CARBON

ALLOTROPES
Allotropes are different physical forms of the same element. The different arrangement of their atoms gives them different appearances and properties.

Diamond

Graphite

GRAPHITE
The atoms form huge sheets. Only weak bonds link the sheets together. Graphite is soft because the sheets can slide over each other easily.

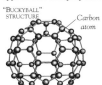

"BUCKYBALL" STRUCTURE

Carbon atom

DIAMOND
Each atom links strongly to four others in a rigid, compact framework that stretches throughout the diamond. This makes the diamond extremely hard.

BUCKMINSTERFULLERENE
The molecules of this newly discovered carbon allotrope have 60 atoms linked in a sphere. It is called a "buckyball".

Carbon atom

MOLECULAR STRUCTURE OF A DIAMOND

Carbon atom

MOLECULAR STRUCTURE OF GRAPHITE

COMPOSITION OF THE EARTH'S CRUST

The bulk of the Earth's crust is oxygen and silicon, mostly combined in rocks or sand (silicon oxide). Clays are made of silicon and oxygen combined with the third most common element – aluminium.

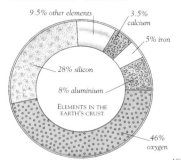

9.5% other elements

3.5% calcium

5% iron

28% silicon

8% aluminium

ELEMENTS IN THE EARTH'S CRUST

46% oxygen

SIMPLEST AND MOST ABUNDANT
Hydrogen and helium, the simplest elements, were the first to form after the Big Bang created the universe. Hydrogen and helium make up 97% of the mass of stars, and are by far the most abundant elements in the universe.

BODY ELEMENTS

The tissues of your body are made up of hydrogen, oxygen, carbon, and nitrogen, while bones contain calcium. Together, these five elements account for 98% of your body mass. Elements such as copper, iron, and zinc occur only in tiny amounts, but these "trace" elements are vital for good health.

Over 50% of your body mass is water

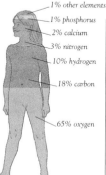

1% other elements

1% phosphorus

2% calcium

3% nitrogen

10% hydrogen

18% carbon

65% oxygen

ELEMENT FACTS

• Ancient Greek philosophers believed there were just four elements: earth, fire, air, and water.

• Astatine is the rarest element on Earth; the rarest metal is rhodium.

• Technetium was the first element to be made artificially.

• Earth's atmosphere is 78% nitrogen.

PERIODIC TABLE

CERTAIN ELEMENTS share similar chemical properties and atomic structures. These similarities become clear when all the known elements are set out in a chart called the periodic table. This chart arranges elements into "groups" (columns) and "periods" (rows).

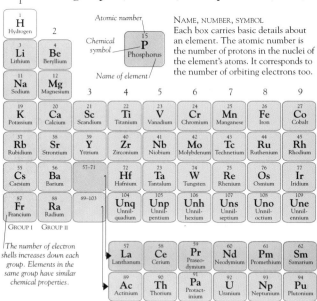

NAME, NUMBER, SYMBOL
Each box carries basic details about an element. The atomic number is the number of protons in the nuclei of the element's atoms. It corresponds to the number of orbiting electrons too.

Atomic number

Chemical symbol

15
P
Phosphorus

Name of element

1								
1 **H** Hydrogen	2							
3 **Li** Lithium	4 **Be** Beryllium							
11 **Na** Sodium	12 **Mg** Magnesium	3	4	5	6	7	8	9
19 **K** Potassium	20 **Ca** Calcium	21 **Sc** Scandium	22 **Ti** Titanium	23 **V** Vanadium	24 **Cr** Chromium	25 **Mn** Manganese	26 **Fe** Iron	27 **Co** Cobalt
37 **Rb** Rubidium	38 **Sr** Strontium	39 **Y** Yttrium	40 **Zr** Zirconium	41 **Nb** Niobium	42 **Mo** Molybdenum	43 **Tc** Technetium	44 **Ru** Ruthenium	45 **Rh** Rhodium
55 **Cs** Caesium	56 **Ba** Barium	57–71	72 **Hf** Hafnium	73 **Ta** Tantalum	74 **W** Tungsten	75 **Re** Rhenium	76 **Os** Osmium	77 **Ir** Iridium
87 **Fr** Francium	88 **Ra** Radium	89–103	104 **Unq** Unnil-quadium	105 **Unp** Unnil-pentium	106 **Unh** Unnil-hexium	107 **Uns** Unnil-septium	108 **Uno** Unnil-octium	109 **Une** Unnil-ennium

GROUP I   GROUP II

The number of electron shells increases down each group. Elements in the same group have similar chemical properties.

57 **La** Lanthanum	58 **Ce** Cerium	59 **Pr** Praseo-dymium	60 **Nd** Neodymium	61 **Pm** Promethium	62 **Sm** Samarium
89 **Ac** Actinium	90 **Th** Thorium	91 **Pa** Protact-inium	92 **U** Uranium	93 **Np** Neptunium	94 **Pu** Plutonium

GROUPS AND PERIODS

Each period starts on the left with a highly reactive alkali metal with an outer shell of one electron. It ends on the right with a stable noble gas in group 18 (0) with eight electrons in its outer shell. Elements in the same group have the same number of electrons in their outer shells.

TYPES OF ELEMENT KEY

- ALKALI METALS
- ALKALINE-EARTH METALS
- TRANSITION METALS
- LANTHANIDES
- ACTINIDES
- POOR METALS
- SEMIMETALS
- NON-METALS
- NOBLE GASES

As the atomic number increases by one along each period, the chemical properties of the element gradually change

18

| 2 **He** Helium |

13 **14** **15** **16** **17**

| 5 **B** Boron | 6 **C** Carbon | 7 **N** Nitrogen | 8 **O** Oxygen | 9 **F** Fluorine | 10 **Ne** Neon |

| 13 **Al** Aluminium | 14 **Si** Silicon | 15 **P** Phosphorus | 16 **S** Sulphur | 17 **Cl** Chlorine | 18 **Ar** Argon |

10 **11** **12**

| 28 **Ni** Nickel | 29 **Cu** Copper | 30 **Zn** Zinc | 31 **Ga** Gallium | 32 **Ge** Germanium | 33 **As** Arsenic | 34 **Se** Selenium | 35 **Br** Bromine | 36 **Kr** Krypton |

| 46 **Pd** Palladium | 47 **Ag** Silver | 48 **Cd** Cadmium | 49 **In** Indium | 50 **Sn** Tin | 51 **Sb** Antimony | 52 **Te** Tellurium | 53 **I** Iodine | 54 **Xe** Xenon |

| 78 **Pt** Platinum | 79 **Au** Gold | 80 **Hg** Mercury | 81 **Tl** Thallium | 82 **Pb** Lead | 83 **Bi** Bismuth | 84 **Po** Polonium | 85 **At** Astatine | 86 **Rn** Radon |

GROUP III GROUP IV GROUP V GROUP VI GROUP VII GROUP 0

Setting the lanthanides and actinides apart from the main table, makes its shape easier to understand

Two alternative number systems are used to group the elements

| 63 **Eu** Europium | 64 **Gd** Gadolinium | 65 **Tb** Terbium | 66 **Dy** Dysprosium | 67 **Ho** Holmium | 68 **Er** Erbium | 69 **Tm** Thulium | 70 **Yb** Ytterbium | 71 **Lu** Lutetium |

| 95 **Am** Americium | 96 **Cm** Curium | 97 **Bk** Berkelium | 98 **Cf** Californium | 99 **Es** Einsteinium | 100 **Fm** Fermium | 101 **Md** Mendelevium | 102 **No** Nobelium | 103 **Lr** Lawrencium |

Elementary data

CHLORINE

Most of the known elements were first identified by scientists during the 18th and 19th centuries, but a few have been known since ancient times. Some can only be produced artifically in a laboratory. Of the 109 elements, all are solids at room temperature, except eleven gases, and mercury and bromine, which are liquids.

SODIUM

POTASSIUM

ELEMENTS PRODUCED ARTIFICIALLY		
ELEMENT	YEAR FIRST MADE	MAKER
Technetium	1937	C. Perrier (France) & E. Segré (Italy/USA)
Astatine	1940	D.R. Corson (USA)
Neptunium	1940	E.M. McMillan & P.H. Abelson (USA)
Plutonium	1944	G. Seaborg (USA)
Americium	1944	G. Seaborg (USA)
Curium	1944	G. Seaborg (USA)
Promethium	1947	J.A. Marinsky (USA)
Berkelium	1949	S.G. Thompson (USA)
Californium	1950	S.G. Thompson and others (USA)
Einsteinium	1952	A. Ghiorso (USA)
Fermium	1952	A. Ghiorso (USA)
Mendelevium	1955	A. Ghiorso (USA)
Nobelium	1958	A. Ghiorso (USA)
Lawrencium	1961	A. Ghiorso (USA)
Unnilquadium	1964	G. Flerov (USSR)
Unnilpentium	1967	A. Ghiorso (USA)
Unnilhexium	1974	A. Ghiorso (USA); G. Flerov (USSR)
Unnilseptium	1976	G. Munzenburg (Germany)
Unnilennium	1982	P. Armbruster (Germany)
Unniloctium	1984	P. Armbruster (Germany)

ANCIENT ELEMENTS	
ELEMENTS	KNOWN SINCE
Carbon	prehistoric times
Sulphur	prehistoric times
Gold	prehistoric times
Lead	prehistoric times
Copper	c.8000 BC
Silver	c.4000 BC
Iron	c.4000 BC
Tin	c.3500 BC
Mercury	c.1600 BC
Antimony	c.1000 BC

BOILING POINTS

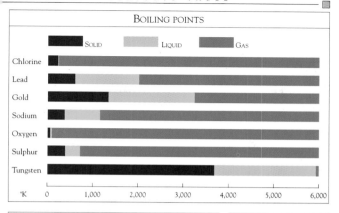

SOLID LIQUID GAS

Chlorine

Lead

Gold

Sodium

Oxygen

Sulphur

Tungsten

°K   0   1,000   2,000   3,000   4,000   5,000   6,000

NAMING ELEMENTS

The names of many elements are derived from Greek words. They give clues about the elements' properties.

ELEMENT/SYMBOL	GREEK WORD	MEANING
Argon (Ar)	Argos	Inactive
Astatine (At)	Astatos	Unstable
Barium (Ba)	Barys	Heavy
Bromine (Br)	Bromos	Stench
Chlorine (Cl)	Chloros	Pale green
Dysprosium (Dy)	Dysprositos	Hard to get
Hydrogen (H)	Hydro genes	Water forming
Mercury (Hg)	Hydragyrum	Liquid silver
Phosphorus (P)	Phosphoros	Bringer of light
Technetium (Tc)	Tekhnetos	Artificial

MORE ELEMENT FACTS

• Helium has the lowest boiling point: −268.93°C (−453.07°F).

• Fluorine gas is the most reactive of all elements.

• At room temperature, osmium is the densest element and lithium the least dense metal. Radon is the densest gas and hydrogen the least dense.

SULPHUR

METALS

MOST ELEMENTS are metals. Many are found in the Earth's crust, combined with other elements as deposits called ores. Metals in their pure form are either not very strong or they rust and tarnish easily. Most of the "metals" we use today are alloys. Alloys are solid mixtures of different metals. They provide hard, strong, long-lasting materials.

COMMON PROPERTIES OF METALS
- Metals have high melting and boiling points.
- They conduct heat and electricity well.
- Metals have a high density, and are malleable (can be beaten) and ductile (can be drawn out into wire).
- Most metals react with air to form oxides, and with acids to release hydrogen.
- Metals form positive ions.

Blacksmith hammers hot iron into shape

ALLOYS

ALLOYS
A metal may be mixed with other metals or non-metals to produce an alloy with more useful properties than the metal alone. The new substance alters the atomic structure of the metal so that the metal's atoms do not move. A tough alloy results.

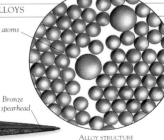

Added atoms

Bronze spearhead

ALLOY STRUCTURE

	COMPOSITION OF COMMON ALLOYS	
ALLOY	TYPICAL COMPOSITION	PROPERTIES
Cast iron	Iron 97%, carbon 3%	Hard but brittle
Duralumin	Aluminium 96%, copper 4%	Strong and light
Pewter	Tin 73%, lead 27%	Fairly soft
Brass	Copper 70%, zinc 30%	Easy to shape
Solder	Tin 50%, lead 50%	Low melting point
Stainless steel	Iron 70%, chromium 20%, nickel 9.5%, carbon 0.5%	Hard and does not rust
Bronze	Copper 70%, tin 30%	Resists corrosion and wear

POOR METALS

A "tin" can may be made of steel coated with tin

Tankard made of pewter, a tin-lead alloy

The poor metals are aluminium, gallium, indium, thallium, tin, lead, bismuth, and polonium. They are softer and weaker than other metals, and melt more easily. Despite their name, they are very useful, especially in making alloys.

SEMIMETALS

Boron, silicon, germanium, arsenic, antimony, selenium, and tellurium are called semimetals because they have some of the properties of metals and some of non-metals. Silicon and germanium are used to make electronic components because they are "semiconductors", that is, they will conduct electricity but only under certain conditions.

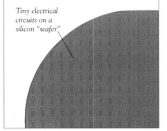

Tiny electrical circuits on a silicon "wafer"

Transition metals

In the middle of the periodic table lies the group of typical metals called the transition metals. They are less reactive than the alkali metals and alkaline-earth metals, and have higher melting and boiling points. Some transition metals, such as copper and nickel, are magnetic.

ZINC
A bluish-grey metal, zinc often provides the casing for batteries. Its main use is as a protective coating that prevents iron or steel from rusting. With copper, it forms the alloy brass. Zinc oxides are used to make rubber and plastic compounds more stable.

NICKEL
Nickel is a shiny metal that does not corrode or tarnish, and neither do its alloys. When alloyed with copper it forms cupronickel, which is used to make coins. In an alloy with chromium, iron, and carbon it produces stainless steel.

SILVER
Apart from jewellery, silver is used mainly in the photographic industry. Black-and-white photographic film is coated with a compound of silver, and either iodine, chlorine, or bromine. The compound is sensitive to light.

Developing the film turns the light-affected areas into pure silver – the dark areas on the negative

IRON
Iron is the most important and cheapest of all the metals we use. However, when exposed to air it oxidizes – that is, it reacts with oxygen in the air to form rust (iron oxide). This problem can be overcome by turning iron into steel.

PLATINUM
Rare and attractive platinum is used in jewellery. It never corrodes or wears away naturally. Platinum's main industrial use is as a catalyst. It is also used in electronic circuits.

MAGNETIC METALS
Iron, cobalt, and nickel are the only transition metals that can be made into strong magnets. The magnetism of an electromagnet can be switched on and off using an electric current.

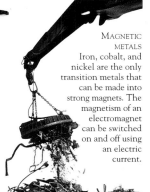

INNER TRANSITION METALS

• The inner transition series consists of the lanthanide and actinide series.

• They are named after the first elements in their series: lanthanum and actinium.

• The lanthanides are so similar that chemists find it difficult to tell them apart.

• All the actinides are radioactive.

URANIUM
Uranium is a radioactive, silvery metal from the actinide series. It is extracted from the ores pitchblende and carnotite. Nuclear reactors use the isotope uranium–235 as a fuel.

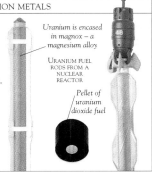

Uranium is encased in magnox – a magnesium alloy

URANIUM FUEL RODS FROM A NUCLEAR REACTOR

Pellet of uranium dioxide fuel

Other metals

At the beginning of the periodic table are two groups of highly reactive metals: the alkali metals and the alkaline-earth metals.

Our bodies need small amounts of some of these – potassium, sodium, magnesium, and calcium – to stay healthy. Francium and radium are radioactive metals.

DANGEROUS METALS

The alkali metals are very reactive. Potassium reacts violently with water, skidding across its surface and creating bubbles of hydrogen gas, which burn with a blue-pink flame. Caesium and rubidium will explode if they touch water.

Potassium reacts violently with water

PROPERTIES OF ALKALI METALS

• The alkali metals are: lithium, francium, potassium, rubidium, sodium, and caesium.

• They form Group 1(I) of the periodic table.

• They are soft enough to cut with a knife.

• They are stored under oil to stop them from reacting with oxygen in the air.

• Their oxides and hydroxides dissolve in water to give strongly alkaline solutions.

• They form ions with a single charge.

• Alkali metals react with some non-metals to form white, soluble, crystalline salts.

• They have low melting points, low boiling points, and low densities compared with other metals.

POTASSIUM FERTILIZER

Plants take in potassium from the soil because it is crucial for their healthy growth. Intensive farming depletes the soil, so farmers must replenish it by adding fertilizers that contain potassium and other nutrients.

SODIUM

Sodium, a silvery, soft alkali metal, tarnishes on exposure to the air. An atom of sodium has 11 electrons, but only one in its outer shell, which makes it very reactive. It is extracted from common salt by electrolysis.

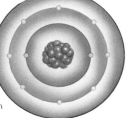

ATOMIC STRUCTURE OF SODIUM

MAGNESIUM

A magnesium atom has 12 electrons, but only two in its outer shell. This makes it reactive, but less so than sodium. Magnesium, a light, alkaline-earth metal, is used in alloys with aluminium and zinc.

ATOMIC STRUCTURE OF MAGNESIUM

PROPERTIES OF ALKALINE-EARTH METALS

• The alkaline-earth metals are: beryllium, magnesium, calcium, strontium, barium, and radium.

• They form Group 2 (II) of the periodic table.

• They react with water to form alkaline solutions. Their compounds are widely found in nature.

• Alkaline-earth metals are reactive, though less so than the alkali metals.

CALCIUM

Calcium is one of the Earth's most abundant metals. There are vast deposits in the form of limestone (also called calcium carbonate). Calcium is also present in bones, teeth, and the shells of molluscs and other sea creatures. The average human contains 1 kg (2.2 lb) of calcium.

RHESUS MONKEY SKELETON

Calcium, in the form of calcium phosphate, gives bone its hardness

NON-METALS

THE NON-METALS are phosphorus, sulphur, hydrogen, carbon, nitrogen, oxygen, the halogens, and the noble gases. Although they form a small part of the periodic table, they are vital to life on Earth. The non-metals include elements that are gases at room temperature (20°C, 68°F) such as hydrogen and oxygen. Solid non-metals include sulphur and phosphorus.

Electron

Proton

HYDROGEN
Hydrogen is at the top of the periodic table because it has the simplest atom, with just one proton orbited by a single electron. It is a colourless, odourless, tasteless, non-toxic gas, and is the least dense of all the elements.

HALOGENS

• The halogens are fluorine, chlorine, bromine, iodine, and astatine.
• They form group 17 (VII) of the periodic table.
• They are all poisonous and have a strong smell.
• Halogens form molecules of two atoms (Cl_2, Br_2, I_2, etc.).
• They react with metals to form salts (such as NaCl, LiF).
• Halogen ions have a single negative charge (F^-, Cl^-, Br^-, I^-, At^-).

NATURAL HALOGENS
The most widespread natural compound containing fluorine is the mineral fluorite (calcium fluoride). Iodine is found in sea water and was once extracted from certain types of seaweed.

Pink fluorite crystal

Laminaria seaweed contains iodine

NOBLE GASES

• The noble gases are helium, neon, argon, krypton, xenon, and radon.

• They form group 18 (0) of the periodic table.

• The noble gases have very low melting and boiling points.

• They all have a full outer shell of electrons, making them extremely unreactive.

• Noble gases exist as single atoms (He, Ne, Ar, Kr, Xe, Rn).

ATOMIC STRUCTURE OF NEON

SAFE GAS
Helium is a light noble gas that is used in balloons and airships. It is very safe to use because it is so unreactive that it cannot catch fire. It is extracted from natural gas wells.

Helium-filled balloons

SWALLOWTAIL BUTTERFLY

CARBON
All life on Earth is based on the element carbon because carbon compounds are vital to the functioning of living cells. Carbon circulates through air, oceans, rocks, and living things in a "carbon cycle".

COMPOSITION OF AIR

Many of the non-metallic elements are present in the air that we breathe.

ELEMENT	PERCENTAGE OF AIR
Nitrogen (N_2)	78%
Oxygen (O_2)	21%
Argon (Ar)	0.93%
Carbon dioxide (CO_2)	0.03%
Neon (Ne)	0.0018%
Helium (He)	0.0005%
Krypton (Kr)	0.00001%
Other gases	0.03769%

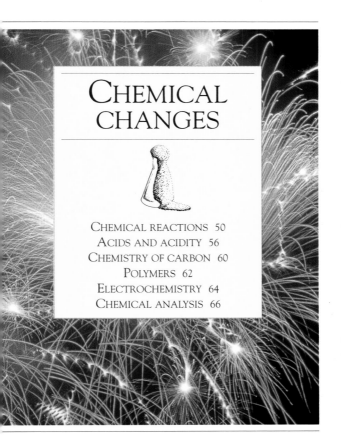

CHEMICAL CHANGES

CHEMICAL REACTIONS

WHEN A CHEMICAL reaction occurs, new substances (called products) form from the substances taking part in the reaction (called reactants). The atoms of the reactants rearrange themselves to form the products.

*As log give.
off heat, th
surroundin.
air become.
hotter*

EXOTHERMIC REACTIONS
Burning is an exothermic reaction – more heat is given out during the reaction than is taken in. Oxidation occurs when a substance combines with oxygen. When a log burns, it combines with oxygen and gives out heat. Reduction occurs when a substance loses oxygen.

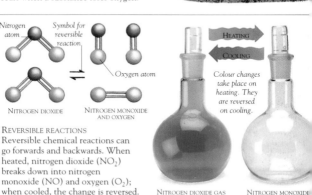

Nitrogen atom

Symbol for reversible reaction

Oxygen atom

NITROGEN DIOXIDE

NITROGEN MONOXIDE AND OXYGEN

HEATING

COOLING

Colour changes take place on heating. They are reversed on cooling.

REVERSIBLE REACTIONS
Reversible chemical reactions can go forwards and backwards. When heated, nitrogen dioxide (NO_2) breaks down into nitrogen monoxide (NO) and oxygen (O_2); when cooled, the change is reversed.

NITROGEN DIOXIDE GAS

NITROGEN MONOXIDE AND OXYGEN GAS

Heat is absorbed during cooking

ENDOTHERMIC REACTIONS

Some reactions take in more heat energy than they give out. These reactions are called "endothermic". When a reaction takes place during cooking, it is endothermic.

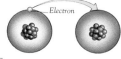

Electron

ELECTRON TRANSFER

During the oxidation process, atoms lose electrons and are "oxidized". During reduction, atoms gain electrons and are "reduced".

ACTIVATION ENERGY

Most reactions need some energy to get them started. This energy is called activation energy. Striking a match gives it the energy to ignite.

Chemicals in match head gain energy

MAKING AND BREAKING BONDS

1 DURING A CHEMICAL REACTION
Energy is taken in when chemical bonds are broken, and it is released when new bonds are formed. When methane (CH_4) burns, it reacts with oxygen (O_2) in the air.

METHANE MOLECULE
Hydrogen atom
Carbon atom

Oxygen atom
Bonds between atoms break
OXYGEN MOLECULES

Bonds will rejoin to form carbon dioxide and water

2 BROKEN BONDS
During the reaction, all the bonds between the atoms are broken. New bonds form as the atoms join up in different combinations.

CARBON DIOXIDE MOLECULE

WATER MOLECULES

3 NEW BONDS FORM
The reaction produces carbon dioxide (CO_2) and water (H_2O). The new bonds have less stored energy than the original ones, so the reaction gives out energy as heat.

Describing reactions

Each element has a chemical symbol to identify it, and each compound a chemical formula. The formula indicates how the elements in the compound are combined. A chemical equation shows which substances react together during a chemical reaction and the products that result.

Lead nitrate solution

Potassium iodide solution

Solid yellow precipitate of lead iodide forms

CHEMICAL EQUATIONS ALWAYS BALANCE
No atoms are lost during a chemical reaction, so its chemical equation must balance, with equal numbers of atoms of each element on either side. Here, lead nitrate solution reacts with potassium iodide solution. The chemical equation for this reaction is shown below.

$$2KI + Pb(NO_3)_2 \longrightarrow PbI_2 + 2KNO_3$$

| Potassium iodide | + | Lead nitrate | $\longrightarrow$ | Lead iodide | + | Potassium nitrate |

Sodium is high in the activity series, and reacts violently with air

REACTION FACTS

• No mass is lost during any chemical reaction – this was first noted by French chemist Antoine Lavoisier in 1774.

• Caesium is the most reactive metal element.

• The present system of using letters to represent elements was devised in 1811.

THE ACTIVITY SERIES
The activity series compares the reactivity of different metals – that is, how readily they form compounds with other substances. Elements at the top of the series are highly reactive. Those at the bottom are very unreactive. Highly reactive metals cannot be found uncombined in nature.

Potassium
Sodium
Calcium
Magnesium
Aluminium
Zinc
Iron
Lead
Copper
Mercury
Silver
Platinum
Gold

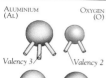

ALUMINIUM
(AL)

OXYGEN
(O)

Valency 3

Valency 2

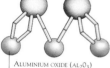

ALUMINIUM OXIDE (AL₂O₃)

*Two aluminium atoms bond
with three oxygen atoms*

VALENCY

An atom's valency shows the number of chemical bonds it can form. It is the number of electrons the atom gains, loses, or shares when it makes bonds. When a compound has formed, the total valencies of the different atoms involved will be the same.

DISPLACEMENT

A metal will displace (put out of place) a less reactive metal from a solution. Here, atoms from a "tree" of copper wire displace silver atoms from a clear solution of silver nitrate. The copper turns the solution blue, while the displaced silver forms crystals on the wire.

*Copper
crystals
grow on the
copper wire*

Copper wire

*Blue copper
nitrate solution
forms*

$$Cu + 2AgNO_3 \longrightarrow Cu(NO_3)_2 + 2Ag$$

Copper + Silver nitrate ⟶ Copper nitrate + Silver

SUFFIXES AND PREFIXES		
SUFFIX	DESCRIPTION	EXAMPLE
-ide	Contains just the two elements in the name	Iron sulphide (FeS)
-ite	Contains oxygen as well as the other elements in the name	Iron sulphite (FeSO₃)
-ate	Contains more oxygen than -ites	Iron sulphate (FeSO₄)
PREFIX	EXAMPLE	ATOMS IN PREFIX
Mono-	Carbon monoxide (CO)	1
Di-	Nitrogen dioxide (NO₂)	2
Tri-	Boron trichloride (BCl₃)	3

Controlling reactions

Chemists speed up reactions by making the reacting particles collide with each other more often or with greater energy. Substances called catalysts speed up reactions by helping substances react together. They remain unchanged by the chemical reaction.

Rate of reaction is slower with a weak dye solution

Strong dye solution reacts faster with material

CONCENTRATION
Increasing the concentration of a reactant speeds up a reaction. Dyeing a material is faster with a concentrated dye – there are more dye molecules to collide with the material.

SURFACE AREA
The surface area of a solid object is the size of its outer surface. Increasing the surface area of a reacting substance speeds up a chemical reaction. This is why chips fry faster than the potato from which they are made. The chips' greater surface area reacts with the hot cooking oil.

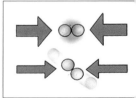

COLLISION THEORY
When particles collide, they usually bounce harmlessly off each other. But if the particles collide with enough force or energy, the bonds holding them together break, and a chemical reaction takes place.

CATALYSTS IN INDUSTRY		
PROCESS	REACTANTS	CATALYST
Manufacture of ammonia	Hydrogen and nitrogen	Iron and iron(III) oxide
Manufacture of nitric acid	Ammonia and oxygen	Platinum
Manufacture of sulphuric acid	Sulphur dioxide and oxygen	Vanadium(V) oxide
Manufacture of margarine	Vegetable oil and hydrogen	Nickel or platinum
Manufacture of methanol	Methane and oxygen	Chromium(III) oxide or zinc oxide

Sugar lump dropped in fizzy drink

SUGAR AS A CATALYST
Sugar makes a fizzy drink fizz harder. It acts as a catalyst for the dissolved carbon dioxide gas to come out of the solution.

CATALYTIC CONVERTER
A car's catalytic converter provides a large surface area for chemical reactions to take place. Harmful gases formed when fuel burns are forced into close contact with catalysts in the converter. The substances react together to produce less harmful gases. The catalysts are unchanged by the reaction.

CATALYTIC CONVERTER

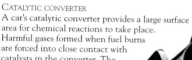

Polluting gases enter converter

Honeycomb structure gives large surface area

Coating of catalysts rhodium and platinum

Gas bubbles make dough expand

Dough is left in warm place

Yeast mixture

NATURAL CATALYSTS
Yeast is a fungus containing enzymes, which are biological catalysts. The enzymes in yeast make starches and sugars break down more rapidly into carbon dioxide gas and ethanol. In bread making, yeast helps the dough to rise.

MORE REACTION FACTS
• Raising temperature or pressure increases the rate of reaction.

• The human body contains over 1,000 different enzymes.

• Biodegradable plastics decompose faster in strong sunlight.

ACIDS AND ACIDITY

STRONG ACIDS are corrosive and burn clothes or skin. However, acids are found in fruit, ants, rain, and even our stomachs. Some acids dissolve metals. The strength of an acid is measured on the pH scale.

CORROSIVE WARNING SYMBOL FOR STRONG ACIDS

Hydrochloric acid poured over metal

Acid reacts furiously with metal chippings, releasing hydrogen gas

Zinc chippings

REACTION OF ACID ON METAL
Hydrochloric acid poured onto zinc chippings causes a fizzing as the hydrogen (present in all acids) is released. The zinc replaces the hydrogen in the solution to form zinc chloride.

ACIDS IN WATER
Water (H_2O) can split into (OH^-) hydroxide and (H^+) hydrogen ions. Acidic compounds add more H^+ ions when they dissolve. A solution's pH is a measure of its H^+ ion concentration.

Water molecule (H_2O)

Hydrogen ion (H^+) splits from water molecule

Hydroxide ion (OH^-)

COMMON ACIDS				
ACID	FORMULA	STRENGTH	pH	OCCURRENCE
Hydrochloric	HCl	Strong	1	Human digestive system
Sulphuric	H_2SO_4	Strong	1–2	Car batteries
Nitric	HNO_3	Strong	1	Industrial processes
Acetic	CH_3COOH	Weak	3–4	Vinegar
Citric	$C_6H_8O_7$	Weak	3	Citrus fruit
Formic	HCOOH	Weak	4.5	Ant bites, nettle stings
Carbonic	H_2CO_3	Weak	4–5	Rainwater, fizzy drinks

UNIVERSAL INDICATOR COLOUR/PH CHART OF ACIDS

1	2	3	4	5	6	7
DIGESTIVE JUICES	CAR BATTERY ACID	LEMON JUICE	VINEGAR	ACID RAIN	TAP WATER	PURE WATER

MEASURING ACIDITY

The pH scale measures acidity (and alkalinity). On the pH scale, 1 is highly acidic, 7 neutral, and 14 highly alkaline. Acidity is measured with indicator papers or solutions, which change colour in acids or alkalis, or with pH meters, which record the concentration of hydrogen ions.

Hydrochloric acid

Indicator paper shows pH of 1

ACID RAIN

Rainwater naturally contains weak carbonic acid, but pollution is now adding sulphuric acid and nitric acid to it. This creates a strong cocktail of acids that can kill trees and aquatic life, and erode statues and buildings.

USES OF SULPHURIC ACID

Sulphuric acid is widely used in industry because it reacts readily with other compounds. It is produced in large quantities after a reaction between sulphur and oxygen.

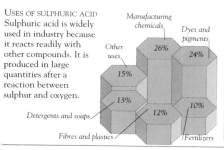

Manufacturing chemicals 26%

Dyes and pigments 24%

Other uses 15%

Detergents and soaps 13%

Fibres and plastics 12%

Fertilizers 10%

ACID FACTS

• pH or "potential of hydrogen", indicates the number of hydrogen ions a substance forms.

• The word "acid" comes from the Latin word for "sour".

• "Heartburn" is caused by excess hydrochloric acid in the stomach.

Alkalis, bases, and salts

BEE

Bases are compounds that cancel out, or neutralize, acidity. When a base reacts with an acid, a substance called a salt is created. Water (H_2O) is also produced. Pure water is neutral: it is neither acidic nor alkaline. Alkalis are bases that are soluble in water.

Painful stings contain acids or alkalis

BEE STINGS AND WASP STINGS
A bee sting is acidic and can be neutralized by a weak alkali such as soap or bicarbonate of soda. Wasp stings are alkaline, so they can be neutralized by a weak acid such as vinegar.

AMMONIA
Fertilizers containing nitrogen are made from the alkali ammonia (NH_3). Ammonia is produced by the Haber process, which causes nitrogen and hydrogen to react together.

WASP

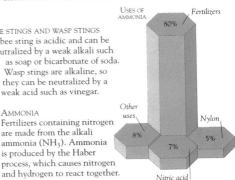

USES OF AMMONIA

Fertilizers 80%

Other uses 8%

Nitric acid 7%

Nylon 5%

COMMON BASES				
BASE	FORMULA	STRENGTH	pH	OCCURRENCE
Sodium hydroxide	NaOH	Strong	14	Soap manufacture
Calcium hydroxide	Ca(OH)$_2$	Strong	12	Neutralizing soil acidity
Ammonium hydroxide solution	NH$_4$OH	Weak	10–11	Household cleaning fluids
Milk of magnesia	Mg(OH)$_2$	Weak	10	Neutralizing stomach acid
Sodium hydrogencarbonate	NaHCO$_3$	Weak	8–9	Bicarbonate of soda
Blood		Weak	7.4	Human body

UNIVERSAL INDICATOR COLOUR/PH CHART OF BASES

7	8	9	10	11	12	13	14
PURE WATER	SOAP	BICARBONATE OF SODA	DISINFECTANT	HOUSEHOLD CLEANER	CALCIUM HYDROXIDE	OVEN CLEANER	SODIUM HYDROXIDE

THE PH OF BASES

The pH scale for bases ranges from neutral pure water (pH 7) to strong alkalis such as sodium hydroxide (pH 14). Soaps are made by making weak organic acids react with a strong base. This makes soaps mildy alkaline, with a pH of 8–9.

Universal indicator paper dipped in calcium hydroxide shows pH of 12

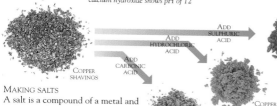

ADD SULPHURIC ACID

ADD HYDROCHLORIC ACID

ADD CARBONIC ACID

COPPER SHAVINGS

COPPER CHLORIDE

COPPER CARBONATE

COPPER SULPHATE

MAKING SALTS

A salt is a compound of a metal and a non-metal joined by ionic bonds. A salt forms when an acid reacts with a base or a metal. Like other metals, copper forms a variety of salts. Making it react with different acids produces very different salts.

CORROSIVE ALKALI WARNING

Alkalis are chemically opposite to acids. They dissolve in water to form negatively charged hydroxide ions (OH⁻), making them as corrosive as acids.

BASE AND SALT FACTS

• In 1908, a German chemist named Fritz Haber devised the manufacturing process for ammonia.

• Alkalis, like acids, are good conductors of electricity. This is because they break up in water to form ions.

CHEMISTRY OF CARBON

THERE ARE MORE than ten million known carbon compounds. All living things contain some compounds of carbon. The study of substances containing carbon is known as organic chemistry.

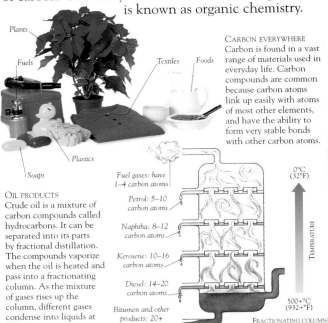

Plants

Fuels

Textiles

Foods

Plastics

Soaps

CARBON EVERYWHERE
Carbon is found in a vast range of materials used in everyday life. Carbon compounds are common because carbon atoms link up easily with atoms of most other elements, and have the ability to form very stable bonds with other carbon atoms.

Fuel gases: have 1–4 carbon atoms

Petrol: 5–10 carbon atoms

Naphtha: 8–12 carbon atoms

Kerosene: 10–16 carbon atoms

Diesel: 14–20 carbon atoms

Bitumen and other products: 20+ carbon atoms

0°C (32°F)

500+°C (932°F)

TEMPERATURE

FRACTIONATING COLUMN

OIL PRODUCTS
Crude oil is a mixture of carbon compounds called hydrocarbons. It can be separated into its parts by fractional distillation. The compounds vaporize when the oil is heated and pass into a fractionating column. As the mixture of gases rises up the column, different gases condense into liquids at different temperatures.

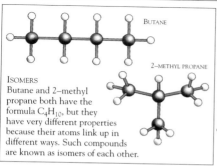

BUTANE

2–METHYL PROPANE

ISOMERS
Butane and 2–methyl
propane both have the
formula C_4H_{10}, but they
have very different properties
because their atoms link up in
different ways. Such compounds
are known as isomers of each other.

AROMATIC COMPOUND
Benzene is a strong-
smelling liquid obtained
from coal. The molecular
structure of benzene – a
ring of six carbon atoms –
is the basis of many useful
"aromatic" compounds.

Hydrogen
atom

MOLECULAR
STRUCTURE
OF BENZENE

Carbon
atom

ORGANIC TERMS		
TERM	MEANING	EXAMPLE
Hydrocarbon	Organic compound of hydrogen and carbon atoms only	Methane (CH_4)
Aromatic	Organic compound with a ring of carbon atoms	Benzene (C_6H_6)
Aliphatic	Organic compound with a chain of carbon atoms	Ethane (C_2H_6)
Alkane	Aliphatic hydrocarbon with single bonds between its carbon atoms	Octane (C_8H_{18})
Alkene	Aliphatic hydrocarbon with a double bond between two of its carbon atoms	Ethene (C_2H_4)
Alkyne	Aliphatic hydrocarbon with a triple bond between two of its carbon atoms	Ethyne (C_2H_2)
Alkyl group	Alkane that has lost one hydrogen atom	Methyl (CH_3–) forms from methane Ethyl (C_2H_5–) forms from ethane
Aryl group	Aromatic compound that has lost one hydrogen atom	Phenyl (C_6H_5–) forms from benzene
Alcohol	Organic compound with a hydroxyl (–OH) group	Ethanol (C_2H_5OH) – ethyl plus a hydroxyl group
Carbohydrate	Organic compound with hydrogen and oxygen atoms in the ratio of 2 to 1	Glucose ($C_6H_{12}O_6$)

POLYMERS

POLYMERS ARE giant
molecules made up of
winding chains of thousands
of smaller molecules called
"monomers". Fats, starches, and
proteins are natural polymers, while
plastics and many artificial fibres are
made from synthetic polymers.

INFLATABLE
PVC (POLYVINYL
CHLORIDE) SNAKE

*PVC is a
"thermoplastic" –
it melts very easily*

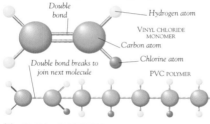

*Double
bond*

Hydrogen atom

VINYL CHLORIDE
MONOMER

*Double bond breaks to
join next molecule*

Carbon atom

Chlorine atom

PVC POLYMER

MONOMERS AND POLYMERS
Vinyl chloride monomers are chemical compounds
of single molecules. They link up end-to-end to form
a long PVC polymer. The double bond in the vinyl
chloride monomer breaks: one bond links to the chain
and the other is able to bond with the next monomer.

*Solutions
react in
beaker*

*Nylon is
drawn out as
a long strand*

MAKING NYLON POLYMERS
Hexanedioic acid and
1,6-diaminohexane react
together to produce nylon.
Their monomers join
up to form long nylon
polymers, which can be
drawn out like thread.

*Rug made from
woollen thread*

NATURAL POLYMERS
Wool and other natural fibres
are made of strong, flexible,
protein polymers. The
fibres are spun
into thread.

TYPES OF POLYMER

POLYMER	PRODUCED FROM	USES
Polythene (polyethylene)	Ethene	Plastic bags, bottles, food wrappings, insulation
Polystyrene	Styrene (phenylethene)	Plastic toys, packaging, insulation, bowls, ceiling tiles
Polyvinyl chloride (PVC)	Vinyl chloride	Guttering and pipes, electrical insulation, waterproof clothing
Acrylic	Derivatives of acrylic acid	Synthetic fibres for clothing, paints
Nylon	Hexanedioic acid and 1,6-diaminohexane	Synthetic fibres for clothing, carpets, plastic ropes, engineering parts
Polyester	Organic acids and alcohols	Fibreglass, synthetic fibres for clothing, boat sails, photographic film
Polymethyl methacrylate (Perspex)	Methyl methacrylate	Glass substitute
Polyurethane	Urethane resins	Packaging foam, adhesives, paints, varnishes
Polytetrafluoroethene (PTFE)	Tetrafluoroethene	Non-stick coating for cooking utensils, artificial body parts, machine bearings
Kevlar	Phenylenediamine, terephthalyl chloride	Bullet-proof vests and other high-strength materials

POLYMERIZING ADHESIVES

The molecules of an adhesive polymerize as they emerge from the tube to form strong bonds between materials. Stabilizing substances stop the adhesive from polymerizing in the tube.

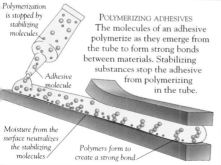

Polymerization is stopped by stabilizing molecules

Adhesive molecule

Moisture from the surface neutralizes the stabilizing molecules

Polymers form to create a strong bond

POLYMER FACTS

• In 1862, English chemist Alexander Parkes made Parkesine, the first plastic.

• Kevlar fibres are stronger than steel, but much lighter.

• There are two types of plastic: thermosets (which do not melt), and thermoplastics (which melt easily).

ELECTROCHEMISTRY

USING ELECTRICITY to break down a substance is called electrolysis. It happens when metal or carbon rods (called electrodes) pass an electric current through a dissolved or molten compound containing ions (called an electrolyte).

Chlorine gas collects in test tube

Electrolyte of copper(II) chloride solution loses its colour

Copper forms at cathode as copper ions gain electrons and become atoms

Chloride ions lose electrons at anode and become atoms of chlorine

ELECTROLYSIS OF COPPER(II) CHLORIDE
Electrolysing a solution of copper(II) chloride ($CuCl_2$) makes copper ions (Cu^{2+}) move to the negatively charged electrode (cathode) where they become copper atoms. Chloride ions (Cl^-) are attracted to the positively charged electrode (anode) where they become chlorine atoms.

BARE NICKEL

SILVER-PLATED

ELECTROPLATING
Using electricity to coat an object with metal is called electroplating. Here, a nickel spoon is plated with silver. Silver ions (Ag^+) in the solution move to the nickel cathode, where they gain electrons and form a deposit of silver. They are replaced by atoms from the silver anode that give up electrons and go into the solution as ions.

Spoon turns in electrolyte of silver nitrate solution

Silver dissolves during electrolysis

FARADAY CONSTANT

The electricity needed to produce 1 mole of an element by electrolysis is always a multiple of 96,500 coulombs. This figure is the Faraday constant (F). The multiple depends on the charge carried by the element's ions.

For example:

1 MOLE OF COPPER
MASS OF 64 GRAMS

• 96,500 (1 x F) coulombs produce 1 mole of iodine (I^-).

• 193,000 (2 x F) coulombs produce 1 mole of copper (Cu^{2+}).

1 MOLE OF IODINE
MASS OF 127 GRAMS

ELECTROLYSIS FACTS

• In 1807, English chemist Humphry Davy discovered the element potassium by electrolysing molten potash (potassium carbonate).

• Electrorefining – using electrolysis to rid a metal of its impurities – can produce copper that is 99.99% pure.

GALVANIZING

A steel car body may be galvanized – that is, given a coating of zinc to guard against rust. The body is electrified and dipped in a bath of an electrolyte containing zinc. The body forms the cathode, so it attracts the zinc ions (Zn^{2+}) in the electrolyte.

Electrons flow towards the copper anode

As the zinc electrode dissolves, electrons flow out of the cell and through the wire

MAKING ELECTRICITY

Chemical reactions can produce an electric current. In this cell, a reaction tears ions (Zn^{2+}) from the zinc plate, leaving it negatively charged. The copper plate loses electrons and becomes positively charged. A current flows as electrons move through the wire to the copper plate.

Electrolyte of dilute sulphuric acid solution

Bulb lit by flow of electrons

CHEMICAL ANALYSIS

CHEMISTS USE various techniques to analyse and identify substances. Qualitative analysis reveals which elements or compounds a substance contains; quantitative analysis shows how much of each element or compound is present.

TITRATION
A sample solution is made to react with a chemical whose concentration is known. When all the solution has reacted, a colour change occurs. Measuring the amount of the chemical used up reveals the concentration of the sample.

The colour of the test solution changes as the pink chemical drops into the flask

PAPER CHROMATOGRAPHY
The ingredients in a dissolved mixture can be revealed by using absorbent paper. The paper takes up different substances at different rates. Black ink, for example, reveals a mixture of dyes.

Dyes travel up paper at different speeds

Blotting paper

Black ink

FLAME TESTS
Metallic elements can be identified by flame tests. A small amount of a metal salt is placed on the end of a platinum wire and heated in a flame. The metal burns and gives the flame a particular colour. Fireworks use metal compounds to produce coloured sparks.

Sodium burns with an orange flame

FLAME TEST FOR IDENTIFYING METALS	
METAL	FLAME COLOUR
Barium	Brown-green
Calcium	Orange-red
Copper	Green-blue
Lithium	Red
Potassium	Lilac
Sodium	Orange

SPECTROSCOPY

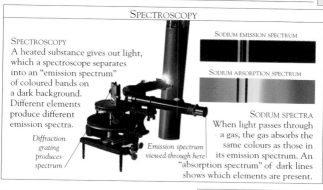

SPECTROSCOPY
A heated substance gives out light, which a spectroscope separates into an "emission spectrum" of coloured bands on a dark background. Different elements produce different emission spectra.

Diffraction grating produces spectrum

Emission spectrum viewed through here

SODIUM EMISSION SPECTRUM

SODIUM ABSORPTION SPECTRUM

SODIUM SPECTRA
When light passes through a gas, the gas absorbs the same colours as those in its emission spectrum. An "absorption spectrum" of dark lines shows which elements are present.

MASS SPECTROSCOPY
Ions of a substance accelerate along a tube. Ions with a particular charge and mass are deflected by a magnetic field so that they strike a detector at the other end of the tube. One by one different ions are detected, producing a mass spectrum.

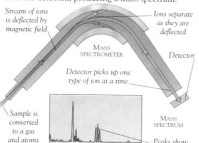

Stream of ions is deflected by magnetic field

Ions separate as they are deflected

MASS SPECTROMETER

Detector

Detector picks up one type of ion at a time

MASS SPECTRUM

Sample is converted to a gas and atoms into ions

Peaks show number of ions

DNA PROFILING
Fragments of the genetic material from skin, blood, or hair roots are analysed using a technique known as electrophoresis. The result is a unique DNA profile that can be used to help identify individual people or animals.

FORCE AND ENERGY

FORCES AT WORK

WHAT MAKES a magnet attract iron filings or an arrow fly towards a target? The answer is force. You cannot see a force, though you feel its effects. Forces push, pull, stretch, or turn an object. Forces are measured in newtons (N).

First component acts along top half of bowstring

Arrow is thrust forwards by resultant force

Second component acts on bottom half of bowstring

COMBINING FORCES

When more than one force acts on an object, the forces (or "components") combine to produce a single force (the "resultant") that acts in one direction only. The force of an arrow fired from a bow is the resultant of component forces acting along the bowstring.

FORCE FACTS

• A jet engine produces a force of at least 200,000 newtons (N).

• Car brakes exert force of up to 5,000 N.

• It takes a force of 5 N to switch on a light.

• To squash an egg requires a force of 50 N.

TORQUE OR TURNING FORCE

Torque is the force that makes an object rotate. It helps a spanner turn a nut. Applying the force far from the nut increases the turning effect. The size of the torque is found by multiplying the force by its distance from the nut.

Extendable spanner

A long handle makes turning the nut easier

BALANCED FORCES

If the forces acting on an object are balanced, the object is said to be in equilibrium. It will either stay at rest, or continue moving at the same speed and in the same direction. These magnets exert exactly equal and opposite forces on the line of ball bearings.

Attraction from north pole of magnet

Equal and opposite component forces mean that the resultant force is zero, so ball bearings remain stationary

Attraction from south pole of magnet

TYPES OF FORCE

- Tension stretches objects.
- Compression squeezes objects.
- Torsion twists objects.
- Shear forces tear objects.
- Centripetal force keeps objects moving in a circle.
- Friction opposes motion.
- Upthrust acts on objects immersed in fluids.

FORCES ON IMMERSED OBJECTS

UPTHRUST IN WATER

Fluids (liquids and gases) exert pressure on immersed objects, producing an upward resultant force called "upthrust". The upthrust equals the weight of the fluid displaced (pushed aside) by the object. In this experiment, the upthrust of the water on the 1 kg mass is 1.2 N.

Displaced water fills pan

Newton balance

1 kg mass

Water weighs 1.2 N

Newton meter reads 8.8 N

Water level rises as object is immersed

Peach displaces water equal to its own weight

FLOATING

If the upthrust on an immersed object is greater than, or equal to, its weight, the object floats. If the upthrust is less than its weight, the object sinks.

The force of gravity

Gravity keeps our feet firmly on the ground. It is a force of attraction between all bodies of matter. All objects experience and exert a certain amount of gravity, depending on their mass. Most people are aware that the Earth's gravity acts on us; few people realize that we pull on the Earth with the same gravitational force.

This apple weighs about 1 N

Mass is the same but weight is different

ON THE MOON

ON EARTH

WEIGHT AND MASS
Weight is the force exerted on an object by gravity. An object's mass is the same on the Moon as it is on Earth, but it weighs less, because the Moon's surface gravity is weaker.

MEASURING FORCE
Gravity pulling on an object creates a force called weight. This force is measured in newtons. A simple instrument that measures force is the newton meter. (A spring balance works in the same way.)

NEWTON'S LAW OF GRAVITATION

According to Newton's law, to find the force of gravity between two objects, you multiply their masses and divide the result by the square of the distance between them. For example, if the Moon was only half as far from Earth, gravity between the two bodies would be four times as strong. If the Moon had twice its mass, the force of gravity between the Moon and Earth would be twice as great.

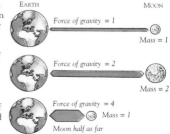

EARTH

MOON

Force of gravity = 1

Mass = 1

Force of gravity = 2

Mass = 2

Force of gravity = 4

Mass = 1

Moon half as far

BALANCING

An object balances easily if it has a low centre of gravity (that is, the point where gravity seems concentrated). Given a slight push, the bottle wobbles but returns to its position; with a high centre of gravity, the same push makes it fall.

Gravity makes near-empty bottle stay upright

Bottle with high centre of gravity falls over

GRAVITY FACTS

• The pull of gravity between the Earth, Moon, and Sun causes the oceans' tides.

• Earth's surface gravity is six times stronger than the Moon's surface gravity.

SI UNITS

The **newton (N)** is the SI unit of force: 1 newton of force causes a mass of 1 kilogram to move with an acceleration of 1 metre per second per second.

EINSTEIN'S GENERAL THEORY OF RELATIVITY

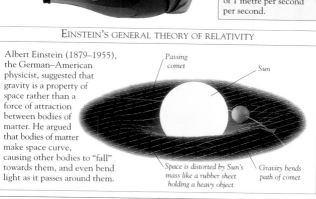

Albert Einstein (1879–1955), the German–American physicist, suggested that gravity is a property of space rather than a force of attraction between bodies of matter. He argued that bodies of matter make space curve, causing other bodies to "fall" towards them, and even bend light as it passes around them.

Passing comet

Sun

Space is distorted by Sun's mass like a rubber sheet holding a heavy object

Gravity bends path of comet

MOTION

FROM TINY PARTICLES to the huge planets, the whole universe is in motion. All objects tend to resist efforts to change their state of motion, whether they are actually moving or at rest. This is called inertia. On Earth, the force of friction causes moving objects to stop, but in space, objects can continue moving forever.

HOW FAST CAN IT GO?

JET AIRCRAFT
3,529 KM/H (2,193 MPH)

POWERBOAT
166 KM/H
(103 MPH)

HIGH-SPEED TRAIN
515 KM/H
(320 MPH)

SPORTS CAR
325 KM/H (202 MPH)

HUMAN
36 KM/H (22 MPH)

CHEETAH
96 KM/H (60 MPH)

SNAIL
0.05 KM/H (0.03 MPH)

Something is described as fast when it has a high speed. In scientific terms, speed has no particular direction. It is simply a measure of how far an object travels in a given time.

VELOCITY
The speed of an object in a particular direction is called its velocity. The velocity of this motorcycle changes as it turns a corner because the direction of motion changes. Its speed remains constant.

If the bike were to continue turning in a circle, it would have a constant speed, but a constantly changing velocity

As the motorcycle turns, its velocity changes

Motorcycle travelling in a straight line at constant velocity

MOTION FACTS
• The Earth travels through space at 107,000 km/h (66,500 mph).
• Earth's gravity accelerates all falling objects at 9.8 m (32.1 ft) per second per second.

ACCELERATION
An object accelerates as its speed increases. Sprinters accelerate most as they pull out of the starting blocks. They decelerate as they cross the finishing line, and their speed decreases.

OVERCOMING INERTIA AND FRICTION

OVERCOMING INERTIA
Pushing the pedals of a bicycle is harder at first, because you need to overcome both your own inertia and that of the bicycle. Once underway, inertia helps to keep you moving.

OVERCOMING FRICTION
Friction tries to oppose motion. It occurs where surfaces or materials rub together. Unless you keep pedalling, friction will bring your bicycle to a halt. Friction also helps the wheels to grip the road.

Friction helps hands grip handlebars

Brakes use friction to stop

Friction helps tyres grip road

Friction helps feet grip pedals

Friction with air slows bicycle and rider

Friction slows pedals and gears

More motion

Not all motion is "linear" (in a straight line). An object may "oscillate" (move back and forth about a fixed point). It may also have circular motion, caused by "centripetal force", which keeps it moving in a circle. Moving objects have "momentum", which is velocity multiplied by mass.

Ball gains momentum when struck by cue

CONSERVATION OF MOMENTUM
When two objects collide, momentum is transferred between them. If a moving snooker ball strikes a stationary one, the first ball transfers some of its momentum to the second ball, which is set in motion. The total momentum of the two balls is the same as it was before the collision.

White ball strikes red ball, transferring momentum

Red ball gains momentum, and moves away

NEWTON'S LAWS OF MOTION

• **First law**
An object will remain at rest or continue travelling at a uniform velocity unless a force acts on it.

• **Second law**
The acceleration of an object is equal to the force acting on it, divided by the object's mass.

• **Third law**
When one object applies a force on another, the second object exerts an equal and opposite force on the first.

Weight is displaced to left

Weight swings towards equilibrium point

OSCILLATING PENDULUM
In an oscillation, such as a pendulum swing, an object is displaced and then pulled back to its equilibrium position (where no resultant force acts on it) by a force (gravity in the case of the pendulum).

Equilibrium point

Momentum takes weight past equilibrium

Athlete pulls on hammer, producing centripetal force

Centripetal force pulls hammer inwards

Hammer's direction changes constantly

Hammer's inertia pulls it outwards

Hammer flies off when released

CIRCULAR MOTION

A whirling object, such as an athletics hammer, tries to fly off in a straight line, but centripetal force pulls the object towards the centre of the circle. This force constantly changes the direction of the object, keeping it moving in a circle.

SPINNING OBJECTS

A spinning object such as a gyroscope has "angular momentum", which gives it stability and makes it resist the force of gravity that tries to topple it. As gravity tries to pull the gyroscope over, its axis moves at right angles to the force of gravity, tracing a small circle.

Guard

Axis traces a circle

Gravity tries to topple gyroscope

Spinning wheel

Axis

GYROSCOPE

MORE MOTION FACTS

• A navigational gyrocompass contains a gyroscope that keeps pointing north once it is set in motion.

• A satellite is kept in a circular orbit by the pull of Earth's gravity, which acts as a centripetal force.

PRESSURE

THE AIR AROUND us presses on us. At the same time, we push on the ground under our feet. Swimmers can feel the surrounding water press on their bodies. This is called pressure. Pressure measures how "concentrated" a force is when it presses on a particular area.

PINPOINT PRESSURE
It is much easier to push a drawing pin into a wall than a thick nail. This is because the drawing pin concentrates all the force exerted by your thumb onto a very small area.

Thumb presses on pin

MEASURING PRESSURE
It is possible to calculate the amount of pressure exerted by dividing the force applied by the area over which it acts. Increasing the area of the surface or reducing the force acting upon it reduces the pressure. Reducing the area or increasing the force acting upon it increases the pressure.

2-kg (20-N) block exerts pressure of 80 Pa

Base covers 0.25 m² (25 squares)

Base covers 0.50 m² (50 squares)

Base covers 0.25 m² (25 squares)

2-kg (20-N) block exerts pressure of 40 Pa

1-kg (10-N) block exerts pressure of 40 Pa

Grid has squares of area 0.01 m²

HOW AN AIRCRAFT FLIES

The curved upper surface of an aircraft's wing makes the air above it travel faster than the air under it. The faster the air moves, the lower its pressure. The difference in pressure creates "lift", a force which pushes the aircraft off the ground.

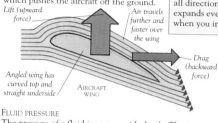

Lift (upward force)

Air travels further and faster over the wing

Drag (backward force)

Angled wing has curved top and straight underside

AIRCRAFT WING

PASCAL'S LAW

Pascal's Law of Fluid Pressures (or Pascal's Principle) states that the pressure is transmitted equally through a fluid (a liquid or a gas) in all directions. This is why a balloon expands evenly in all directions when you inflate it with air.

SI UNITS

The **pascal** (Pa) is the SI unit of pressure: 1 pascal is equal to a force of 1 newton applied to an area of 1 square metre ($1 N/m^2$).

FLUID PRESSURE

The pressure of a fluid increases with depth. This is why pressures in the deepest oceans are greater than they are just below the surface. Below, holes at different depths allow coloured water out at different pressures.

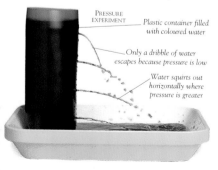

PRESSURE EXPERIMENT

Plastic container filled with coloured water

Only a dribble of water escapes because pressure is low

Water squirts out horizontally where pressure is greater

PRESSURE FACTS

• The pressure at the bottom of the deepest ocean is 1.1×10^8 Pa.

• Standard atmospheric pressure at sea level is 101,325 Pa.

• Sharper knives cut better than blunt ones because their blades exert more pressure.

• Snowshoes help you walk on snow, spreading the weight and reducing the pressure underfoot.

SIMPLE MACHINES

MACHINES CAN CHANGE the direction or size of a force. For example, an axe is a machine called a wedge that splits a log easily. The effort used to wield the axe is sent a long way into the log, pushing it apart a short distance with a greater force.

Axe blade is a wedge

AXE SPLITTING A LOG

SCREW

Turning effort

Turning the head of the screw moves the whole screw forwards with a greater force than is used to turn it.

Total length of screw thread

Effort applied to rim is magnified by axle

WHEEL AND AXLE

Applying a small effort to the rim of the wheel makes the axle turn with a greater force. A large effort at the axle means that the rim turns with less force, but travels further.

INCLINED PLANE

An inclined plane is a slope that reduces the effort required to move an object. For example, pulling a car up a ramp is easier than lifting it vertically. The car must travel further, but less effort is needed to move it.

Force of tension in rope pulls car up slope

A winch is a form of wheel and axle

Winch magnifies force applied to handle

Car travels further than if lifted vertically

Weight of car pulls downwards

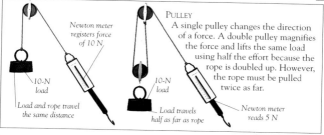

Newton meter
registers force
of 10 N

10-N
load

Load and rope travel
the same distance

PULLEY

A single pulley changes the direction of a force. A double pulley magnifies the force and lifts the same load using half the effort because the rope is doubled up. However, the rope must be pulled twice as far.

10-N
load

Load travels
half as far as rope

Newton meter
reads 5 N

SIMPLE LEVER

A lever is a bar that exerts a force by turning on a pivot, or "fulcrum". A small effort moved through a greater distance at one end moves a larger load through a shorter distance at the other end.

Small force
is applied

Direction of
movement

Large load
is moved

Lever
magnifies
force

Fulcrum

MACHINE EQUATIONS

A machine's force ratio shows how effective the machine is as a force magnifier. The velocity ratio shows how effective the machine is as a distance magnifier.

$$\text{Force ratio} = \frac{\text{load}}{\text{effort}}$$

$$\text{Velocity ratio} = \frac{\text{distance moved by effort}}{\text{distance moved by load}}$$

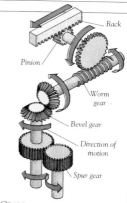

Rack

Pinion

Worm
gear

Bevel gear

Direction
of motion

Spur gear

GEARS

Intermeshing toothed wheels and bars that transmit force and motion are called gears. They can alter the force's size, and the motion's speed and direction.

ENERGY

EVERYTHING WE DO is fuelled by energy.
Our energy comes from food, which
contains chemical energy stored in
chemical compounds. Light, sound,
heat, and electricity are forms of energy.
Movement energy is called kinetic energy.

If the kitten falls, it will have kinetic energy

Box has kinetic energy when opened

POTENTIAL ENERGY
An object gains
potential energy if
it is squeezed or
stretched; the energy
is stored until the
object is released.
The coiled spring
of a jack-in-the-
box has potential
energy. When the
box is opened and
the jack leaps out, the
energy becomes kinetic energy.

GRAVITATIONAL POTENTIAL
A raised object has
gravitational potential
energy – the potential to
fall back to Earth. If the
kitten loses its grip, this
energy converts to kinetic
energy as the kitten
tumbles to the ground.

ENERGY FACTS

• There are about
1,000 million million
joules of heat and
potential energy in
a thunderstorm.

• A teenage girl needs
about 10,000 kJ of
energy each day.

CHEMICAL ENERGY
When we digest
food, chemical
compounds in the
food are broken down and
energy is released for our
bodies to use. Different
foods contain different
amounts of energy. This
chocolate has as much
energy as all these tomatoes.

24 g (0.8 oz) of milk chocolate

1 kg (2.2 lb) of tomatoes

ENERGY USE	
ACTIVITY BY 70-KG PERSON	ENERGY USED IN JOULES PER SECOND (J/S)
Sleeping	60
Sitting reading	120
Playing the piano	160
Walking slowly	250
Running or swimming	800
Walking up stairs	800

SI UNITS

The **joule** (J) is the SI unit of energy and work: 1 joule of energy is used when a force of 1 newton moves through a distance of 1 metre. A kilojoule (kJ) is 1,000 J.

The **hertz** (Hz) is the SI unit of wave frequency: 1 hertz is one complete wave, or vibration, per second. A kilohertz (kHz) is 1,000 Hz.

WAVE ENERGY

TYPES OF WAVES

Energy often travels as moving vibrations called waves. Light and other forms of electromagnetic radiation travel as transverse waves: the vibration is at right angles to the wave's direction. Sound waves travel as longitudinal waves: the vibration is in the same direction as the wave.

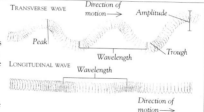

TRANSVERSE WAVE
Direction of motion →
Amplitude
Peak
Wavelength
Trough

LONGITUDINAL WAVE
Wavelength
Direction of motion →

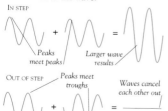

IN STEP

Peaks meet peaks
+
Larger wave results
=

OUT OF STEP
Peaks meet troughs
+
Waves cancel each other out
=

INTERFERENCE

When waves meet, they "interfere" with each other. If two waves are in step, their peaks coincide and they combine to form a bigger wave (constructive interference). If the waves are out of step, the troughs cancel out the peaks and there is no resulting wave (destructive interference).

Work, power, efficiency

Work is done when a force moves something.
Work cannot be done without energy. Energy
provides the ability to do work. When work is
done, energy converts from one form to another.
The rate at which work is done, or energy changed
from one form to another, is called power.

*Total weight
is 400 N*

*Bar carries two
sets of 200-N
weights*

*Weights are
raised about
1.5 m (4.9 ft)*

WEIGHTLIFTER
RAISING
WEIGHTS

*Raised weights
have gravitational
potential energy*

*Weightlifter raises
weights in two seconds*

WORK AND POWER
When this man raises
a heavy weight, the power of
lifting the weight is calculated
by multiplying the weight by
the height to which it is raised
and dividing the result by the
time taken to lift it. So if he lifts
400 newtons by 1.5 metres in
two seconds, the power is 300 W.

SI UNITS

The **watt** (W) is the SI
unit of power: 1 W is
the conversion of 1
joule of energy from
one form to another in
1 second. A kilowatt
(kW) is 1,000 watts,
and a megawatt (MW)
is 1,000,000 W.

The **kilowatt-hour**
(kWh) measures
electrical energy use:
1 kWh is energy used
when a 1-kW appliance
runs for 1 hour.

WORK FACTS

• The efficiency of
a 100-watt light bulb
is 15%, because 85
joules in every 100
are lost as heat.

• The first internal
combustion engine was
built by Étienne Lenoir,
a Belgian engineer.

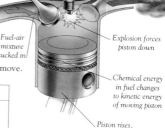

ENERGY CONVERSION

Machines are really "energy converters": they change energy from one form to another to do work. A car is powered by an internal combustion engine, which burns petrol or diesel fuel. The chemical energy in the fuel is converted to the kinetic energy of moving pistons, which make the car move.

Fuel-air mixture sucked in

Explosion forces piston down

Chemical energy in fuel changes to kinetic energy of moving piston

Piston rises, expelling waste gases, and process starts again

INTERNAL COMBUSTION ENGINE

EFFICIENCY

Efficiency tells you how good a machine is as an energy converter. It compares the energy you put into a machine to the energy you get out of it.

MACHINE		ENERGY OUTPUT (% OF INPUT)
Car petrol engine	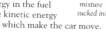	15%
Rocket		about 15%
Steam train		15%
Jet engine		20%
Diesel train		35%
Electric train		35%
Coal-fired power station		35%
Wind farm		about 40%
Magnetic levitation train		about 60%
Hydroelectric plant		80%
Bicycle		90%

LAW OF CONSERVATION OF ENERGY

Energy can neither be created nor destroyed. The Law of Conservation of Energy states that energy can be converted into different forms, but the total amount of energy always stays the same. This law applies even to nuclear reactions, such as those that occur at the core of the Sun.

ENERGY EQUATIONS

Work (joules) = force (newtons) x distance moved (metres)

Power (watts) = $\dfrac{\text{work done (joules)}}{\text{time taken (seconds)}}$

Efficiency (%) = $\dfrac{\text{energy (or power) in}}{\text{energy (or power) out}} \times 100$

HEAT AND TEMPERATURE

THE MORE ENERGY an object's particles have, the hotter the object is. Heat is the total kinetic energy of an object's moving particles. Temperature is a measure of the average kinetic energy of the particles.

Height of liquid shows temperature

Liquid-crystal display

Heat-sensitive resistor in tip

THERMOMETERS
Everyday thermometers measure temperature on the Celsius and Fahrenheit scales. Liquid thermometers use a column of mercury or alcohol that expands as the temperature rises. An electronic thermometer measures temperature with a tiny, heat-sensitive resistor.

Meter records temperature of filament

PYROMETER
A pyrometer measures high temperatures. When pointed at a hot, glowing object, an electric current heats a filament until the colour matches that of the object. Measuring the electric current reveals the temperature.

Light from glowing object

Electric filament is heated until its colour matches light from hot object

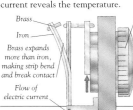

Brass

Iron

Brass expands more than iron, making strip bend and break contact

Flow of electric current

Temperature selector

THERMOSTAT
A thermostat regulates temperature using a "bi-metallic strip" made of brass and iron. The metals expand at different rates, so the strip bends as it heats up. At the required temperature, the strip breaks an electrical contact and turns off a heater.

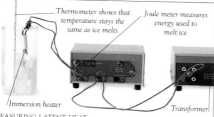

Thermometer shows that temperature stays the same as ice melts

Joule meter measures energy used to melt ice

Immersion heater

Transformer

SI UNITS

The **kelvin** (K) is the SI unit of temperature. There are no minus values on the kelvin scale. This is because 0 K is "absolute zero" – the lowest possible temperature, at which the motion of all particles would cease. Absolute zero has never been attained.

MEASURING LATENT HEAT

This experiment measures the heat needed to melt ice. As a substance changes state, for example, from solid to liquid, it takes in or gives out heat without changing its temperature. This hidden heat is called "latent" heat.

RANGE OF TEMPERATURES	
TEMPERATURE	EXAMPLE
14 million K (14 million°C; 25 million°F)	Sun's core
30,000 K (29,727°C; 53,540°F)	Lightning bolts
5,800 K (5,527°C; 9,980°F)	Surface of the Sun
4,000 K (3,727°C; 6,740°F)	Core of the Earth
523 K (250°C; 482°F)	Burning point of wood
373 K (100°C; 212°F)	Boiling point of water
331 K (58°C; 136°F)	Highest recorded air temperature on Earth
310 K (37°C; 98.6°F)	Normal human body temperature
273 K (0°C; 32°F)	Freezing point of water
184 K (−89°C; −128°F)	Lowest recorded air temperature on Earth
43 K (−230°C; −382°F)	Surface temperature of Pluto (most distant planet)
0 K (−273.15°C; −459.67°F)	Absolute zero

SPECIFIC HEAT CAPACITIES

Specific heat capacity (symbol c) is the amount of heat energy needed to raise the temperature of 1 kilogram of a substance by 1 kelvin (or 1°C).

SUBSTANCE	SPECIFIC HEAT CAPACITY (J/kg/K)
Water	4,200
Alcohol	2,400
Ice	2,100
Nylon	1,700
Marble	880
Concrete	800
Glass	630
Steel	450
Copper	380
Lead	130

Heat transfer

Heat energy always passes from hot
objects or materials to cooler ones. Heat
travels through solids by a process called
conduction, and through fluids (liquids
and gases) by convection. Matter can
also lose or gain heat energy by radiation.

*Swirling colour trails show how
heat spreads through liquid*

CONVECTION IN WATER
The hot, coloured water is less dense
than the cold water surrounding it. The
hot water floats to the surface and loses
heat to the air. As it cools it sinks once
more. This circulation, or "convection
current", spreads heat through the liquid.

*Hot,
coloured
water floats
to the top
of the jar*

*Bottle
contains hot,
coloured
water*

*Thermometer
reads 18.7°C*

*Metal block at
room temperature*

MEASURING HEAT RADIATION
At room temperature, all objects emit infrared
radiation: hotter objects emit more radiation
than cooler ones. The lamp in the picture
emits a lot of radiation, which travels through
the air and heats the metal block below.

*Radiation from lamp absorbed
by particles in metal block*

Desk lamp

*Thermometer
reads 31°C*

*Heat from feet
conducts into stone,
leaving feet feeling cold*

CONDUCTION
When one part of a
substance is heated, its
particles vibrate faster.
They "conduct" (pass
on their heat energy)
as they knock against
neighbouring particles.

CELSIUS & FAHRENHEIT

Temperatures are usually given in degrees Celsius (°C) or Fahrenheit (°F). The Celsius scale is based on the freezing point of water (0°C/32°F) and the boiling point of water (100°C/212°F). The kelvin scale is used in scientific work.

THERMAL CONDUCTIVITY

Thermal conductivity tells you the rate of transfer of heat. Here, the temperature of a material is raised through 1 m by 1 K (or 1°C).

SUBSTANCE	CONDUCTIVITY (W/m/K)	
Copper	385	Good conductor
Gold	296	
Iron	72	
Glass	1	
Brick	0.6	
Water	0.6	
Nylon	0.25	
Wood (oak)	0.15	Bad conductor
Concrete	0.1	
Wool	0.040	
Air	0.025	

INSULATORS

Materials that are poor conductors of heat are called insulators. They include plastics, wood, cork, fibreglass, and air. Architects and builders use insulators in houses and offices to reduce the loss of heat through walls, roofs, ceilings, windows, and floors. A good insulating material is said to have a very low "U-value".

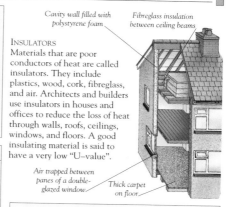

Cavity wall filled with polystyrene foam

Fibreglass insulation between ceiling beams

Air trapped between panes of a double-glazed window

Thick carpet on floor

U-VALUES (FOR HEAT CONDUCTION)

U-value (W/m²/K) is a measure of the rate of heat flow in watts (W) per square metre (m²) of a material so that its temperature increases 1 K (or 1°C).

MATERIAL	U-VALUE (W/m²/K)
Roof with no insulation	2.2
Insulated roof	0.3
Single brick wall	3.6
Double brick wall, air cavity between	1.7
Double brick wall filled with foam	0.5
Single-glazed window	5.6
Double-glazed window with air gap	2.7
Floor without carpets	1
Floor with carpets	0.3

ENERGY SOURCES

MOST OF THE WORLD'S electricity is generated by burning fossil fuels. But there are limited supplies of these fuels and they are only replaced over many millions of years. In the future, we will have to rely on renewable sources, such as wind and solar power, and hydroelectricity.

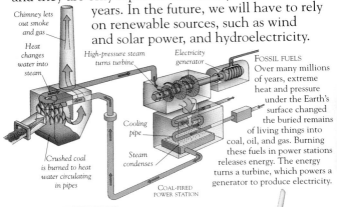

Chimney lets out smoke and gas

Heat changes water into steam

High-pressure steam turns turbine

Electricity generator

Crushed coal is burned to heat water circulating in pipes

Cooling pipe

Steam condenses

COAL-FIRED POWER STATION

FOSSIL FUELS
Over many millions of years, extreme heat and pressure under the Earth's surface changed the buried remains of living things into coal, oil, and gas. Burning these fuels in power stations releases energy. The energy turns a turbine, which powers a generator to produce electricity.

ENERGY SOURCE FACTS

• Hydroelectricity supplies about 3% of the world's energy needs.

• One gram of coal contains about 25 kJ of energy, and one gram of oil about 45 kJ.

• Most people in the world still use firewood.

WIND POWER
A wind turbine is a tall tower with large rotating blades that harness the wind's kinetic energy to produce electricity. A "wind farm" is a large group of wind turbines.

Blades can be up to 20 m (65 ft) long

As the blades turn in the wind, they power an electricity generator

Lightning conductor

Tower

HYDROELECTRIC POWER

Hydroelectricity is an efficient, pollution-free energy source. A hydroelectric power station is situated below a dam at the head of a reservoir. Water rushing down from above turns the power station's turbines at great speed. The turbines are connected to generators that produce electricity.

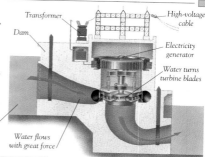

Transformer

High-voltage cable

Dam

Electricity generator

Water turns turbine blades

Water builds up behind dam at end of reservoir

Water flows with great force

SOLAR POWER

Solar cells transform the energy of sunlight into electricity. To generate useful amounts of electricity, solar power stations use hundreds of large mirrored panels that concentrate sunlight onto large solar cells.

ENERGY SOURCES THROUGH TIME

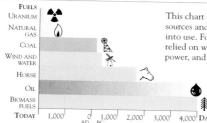

FUELS						
URANIUM						
NATURAL GAS						
COAL						
WIND AND WATER						
HORSE						
OIL						
BIOMASS FUELS						
TODAY	1,000	0	1,000	2,000	3,000	4,000	DATE
		AD BC				

This chart shows when different energy sources and technologies first came into use. For most of history, people relied on wind, water, and muscle power, and burned biomass fuels, (such as wood). Today, non-renewable energy sources, such as coal and oil, are much more commonly used.

Nuclear energy

Atoms are tiny storehouses of energy. This energy comes from strong forces that hold the particles in the centre, or nucleus, of an atom. Tremendous "nuclear" energy can be released when the nucleus of an atom splits (fission), or when two nuclei fuse together (fusion). Nuclear reactors harness this energy to produce electricity.

INTERNATIONAL WARNING SYMBOL FOR RADIOACTIVITY

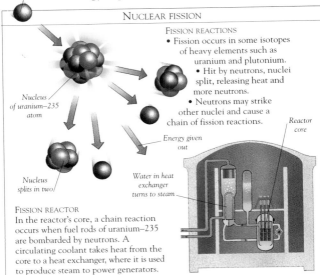

NUCLEAR FISSION

Neutron

FISSION REACTIONS
• Fission occurs in some isotopes of heavy elements such as uranium and plutonium.
• Hit by neutrons, nuclei split, releasing heat and more neutrons.
• Neutrons may strike other nuclei and cause a chain of fission reactions.

Nucleus of uranium–235 atom

Nucleus splits in two

Energy given out

Reactor core

Water in heat exchanger turns to steam

FISSION REACTOR
In the reactor's core, a chain reaction occurs when fuel rods of uranium–235 are bombarded by neutrons. A circulating coolant takes heat from the core to a heat exchanger, where it is used to produce steam to power generators.

NUCLEAR FUSION

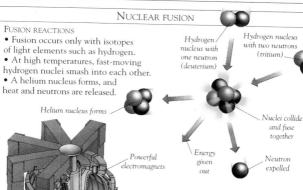

FUSION REACTIONS

• Fusion occurs only with isotopes of light elements such as hydrogen.
• At high temperatures, fast-moving hydrogen nuclei smash into each other.
• A helium nucleus forms, and heat and neutrons are released.

Hydrogen nucleus with one neutron (deuterium)

Hydrogen nucleus with two neutrons (tritium)

Helium nucleus forms

Nuclei collide and fuse together

Energy given out

Neutron expelled

Powerful electromagnets

Plasma circulates in the torus

FUSION REACTOR

A practical fusion reactor has not yet been built. Experimental "tokamak" reactors contain a circular tube or "torus". Fusion occurs in the tube when hydrogen plasma is heated to very high temperatures. Powerful electromagnets confine the plasma.

NUCLEAR WEAPONS

The violent power of nuclear weapons comes from a fission or fusion reaction. The nuclear reaction in the bomb changes a tiny amount of mass into a vast amount of destructive energy.

Mushroom-shaped cloud of smoke and flames

NUCLEAR FACTS

• The first nuclear reactor was built by the physicist Enrico Fermi in the USA in 1942.

• Nuclear fusion occurs in the heart of the Sun and other stars.

• The USA has the most nuclear reactors (109) in the world.

LIGHT

ELECTROMAGNETIC RADIATION

LIGHT IS ONE of several types of wave energy called electromagnetic radiation. This radiation also includes radio waves, microwaves, infrared rays, ultraviolet rays, X-rays, and gamma rays. Together, they form the electromagnetic spectrum.

ELECTROMAGNETIC RADIATION AS WAVES AND PARTICLES

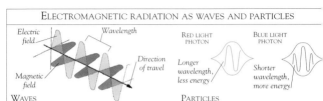

Electric field

Wavelength

Direction of travel

Magnetic field

RED LIGHT PHOTON

BLUE LIGHT PHOTON

Longer wavelength, less energy

Shorter wavelength, more energy

WAVES
Electromagnetic radiation travels as waves of oscillating (fluctuating) electric and magnetic fields. These are at right angles to each other and to the direction of travel.

PARTICLES
Electromagnetic radiation also travels as a stream of particles called photons – tiny "energy packets" given off when charged particles lose energy.

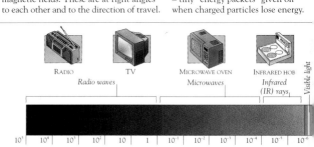

RADIO

TV

MICROWAVE OVEN

INFRARED HOB

Visible light

Radio waves

Microwaves

Infrared (IR) rays

| 10^5 | 10^4 | 10^3 | 10^2 | 10 | 1 | 10^{-1} | 10^{-2} | 10^{-3} | 10^{-4} | 10^{-5} | 10^{-6} |

TABLE OF USEFUL X-RAYS

WAVELENGTH (M) OF X-RAYS	USES AND APPLICATIONS
3×10^{-13}	Killing deep cancer tumours
3×10^{-12}	Inspecting welded joints in steel pipes
1.8×10^{-11}	Diagnostic chest X-rays
6×10^{-9}	Treatment of skin diseases

COMMON PROPERTIES OF ELECTROMAGNETIC WAVES

All types of electromagnetic radiation:

- Transfer energy from place to place

- Can be emitted and absorbed by matter

- Do not need a material medium to travel through

- Travel at 3×10^8 m/s in a vacuum

- Are transverse waves

- Can be polarized

- Can produce interference effects

- Can be reflected and refracted

- Can be diffracted

- Carry no electric charge.

FILTERED LIGHT

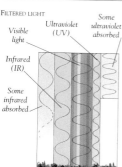

Visible light

Ultraviolet (UV)

Some ultraviolet absorbed

Infrared (IR)

Some infrared absorbed

FILTERED LIGHT
Electromagnetic radiation reaches us from the Sun, stars, and galaxies. The Earth's atmosphere absorbs most types of electromagnetic radiation, but allows radio waves and light to pass through. Some wavelengths of IR and UV are filtered out before reaching the ground.

UV SUNBED
Ultraviolet (UV) rays

X-RAY MACHINE
X-rays

NUCLEAR EXPLOSION
Gamma rays

ELECTROMAGNETIC SPECTRUM

Waves at this end of the spectrum have more energy

| 10^{-9} | 10^{-10} | 10^{-11} | 10^{-12} | 10^{-13} | 10^{-14} | 10^{-15} | 10^{-16} | 10^{-17} |

WAVELENGTH (IN METRES)

LIGHT SOURCES

LIGHT IS A FORM of energy. It is produced
by two processes – incandescence
and luminescence. Incandescence
is the emission of light by hot
objects. Luminescence is
the emission of light
without using heat.

*Electron gives out photon as
it falls back to its original orbit*

LIGHT FROM THE SUN

Most of the light that reaches
us from space comes from the
Sun. Light is produced in the
Sun by incandescence. The light
travels through space at 299,792.5 km
per second (186,282.4 miles per second).

PHOTONS

If an atom gains energy, electrons
orbiting the nucleus jump to higher
orbits, or "energy levels". When the
electrons return to their original
orbits, they release photons of light,
or other electromagnetic radiation.

LUMINESCENCE

TYPE	EXAMPLE	
Triboluminescence Light released by friction	When some crystals, such as sugar, are suddenly crushed, the friction makes them briefly emit light.	
Bioluminescence The emission of light without heat by living organisms	Creatures such as fireflies have chemicals in their bodies that combine to release light energy.	
Phosphorescence The gradual emission of stored energy as light	Glow-in-the-dark paints absorb light energy and release it slowly. The light energy is especially noticeable in the dark.	
Fluorescence The rapid re-emission of light energy	Fluorescent dyes often contain fluorescent chemicals that briefly absorb ultraviolet light and then emit it as visible light.	

INCANDESCENCE

An incandescent bulb contains a thin filament of tungsten wire. An electric current heats the filament so that it glows white and gives off light. The bulb is filled with an unreactive gas such as argon to stop the filament burning up, as it would do in air.

Glowing filament

Unreactive gas

Bulb screws into electrical socket

LIGHT SOURCE FACTS

• Fireflies produce light to attract mates.

• Prehistoric peoples used stone lamps that burned animal fat.

• Laser stands for "Light Amplification by Stimulated Emission of Radiation".

Light reflects up and down tube

Beam leaves through partly silvered mirror

Power supply

Photons of light

LASER LIGHT

A laser produces pure light of intense heat and energy. Light from a coiled tube "excites" atoms in a central tube of "lasing medium". The light that these "excited" atoms produce is reflected between the tube's mirrored ends, escaping as an intense laser beam.

SI UNITS

• The **candela** (cd) is the SI unit of brightness (luminous intensity). A light source of 1 candela is approximately equal to the brightness of a burning candle.

• The **lux** (lx) is the SI unit of illumination. A 1-candela light source gives an illumination of 1 lux to a surface of 1 m² (10.8 sq ft) at a distance of 1 m (3.28 ft).

DISCHARGE TUBE

A discharge tube is a gas-filled tube fitted with two electrodes. When a powerful electric current flows between the electrodes, the vapour gives out, or "discharges", light. Most street lamps use sodium vapour discharge tubes.

Sodium vapour in discharge tube glows with yellow-orange light

Electrode

SODIUM VAPOUR LAMP

LIGHT AND MATTER

A MATERIAL appears shiny, dull, or clear depending on whether it reflects, absorbs, or transmits light rays. Light may bend as it passes through materials, creating optical illusions such as mirages.

Transparent (clear)

Translucent (milky)

Opaque (dull)

Reflective (shiny)

LIGHT PASSING THROUGH MATTER

Light passes through transparent materials. Opaque materials block light. Translucent materials let light through, but scatter it. Light rays bounce off the surface of reflective materials.

REFRACTIVE INDEX

When a light ray passes through a material, its speed changes. If it enters the material at an angle, the difference in speed "refracts", or bends, the light ray. The refractive index shows how much a material reflects light:

Refractive = Speed of light in vacuum
index   Speed of light in material

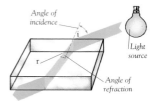

Angle of incidence

Light source

Angle of refraction

MATERIAL	REFRACTIVE INDEX	SPEED OF LIGHT (KM/S)
Air	1.00	300,000 (186,000 miles)
Water	1.33	225,000 (140,000 miles)
Perspex	1.40	210,000 (130,000 miles)
Glass (variable)	1.60	185,000 (115,000 miles)
Diamond	2.40	125,000 (78,000 miles)

The refractive index can also be calculated from the angles in the diagram, using an equation known as Snell's Law:

Refractive = Sin i
index   Sin r

INTERNAL REFLECTION OF LIGHT

If a light ray enters a material at a shallow enough angle (called the "critical angle"), it is refracted so much that it does not emerge from the material, but is reflected inside it.

INTERNAL REFLECTION	
SUBSTANCE	CRITICAL ANGLE
Water	49°
Glass	42°
Diamond	24°

Rays hit sides at shallow angle

No light escapes as ray is reflected

Ray hits end of bar at steep angle

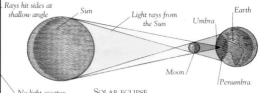

Sun

Light rays from the Sun

Earth

Umbra

Moon

Penumbra

SOLAR ECLIPSE

During a solar eclipse, the Moon, because it is opaque, casts a shadow over the Earth. No rays reach the shadow's centre (umbra); some rays reach its outer area (penumbra).

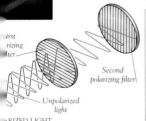

First polarizing filter

Second polarizing filter

Unpolarized light

POLARIZED LIGHT

Light rays vibrate in many different planes. A polarizing filter only allows light vibrating in one plane to pass. A second filter can be used to block out the remaining light. Sunglasses may use polarizing filters to cut out glare.

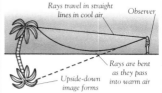

Rays travel in straight lines in cool air

Observer

Rays are bent as they pass into warm air

Upside-down image forms

MIRAGE

Light is refracted as it passes through layers of air at different temperatures. Light rays travelling from the palm tree to the ground are bent upwards by the warm air so that it seems to an observer that the tree has a watery reflection.

LENSES AND MIRRORS

LENSES ARE CURVED transparent materials that make
light rays converge (come together) or diverge (spread
out). Mirrors are shiny materials that reflect light.
Curved mirrors can
also make light rays
converge or diverge.

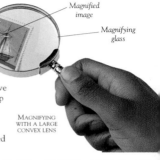

Magnified image

Magnifying glass

MAKING LARGER

This stamp looks much bigger when an
outwardly curving convex lens is held above
it. The lens bends light rays from the stamp
inwards before they reach your eyes. Your
brain assumes that the rays have travelled
in a straight line, as if they were coming
from a much larger stamp. The more curved
a lens, the more it magnifies an object.

MAGNIFYING
WITH A LARGE
CONVEX LENS

MAKING SMALLER

An inwardly curving concave
lens gives a reduced image of
the squares. It makes light
rays from the squares spread,
but your brain assumes they
have travelled in a straight
line, as if they were coming
from much smaller squares.

CONVEX AND CONCAVE LENSES

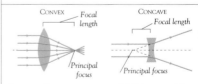

CONVEX — Focal length

CONCAVE — Focal length

Principal focus

Principal focus

A convex lens converges parallel light rays at the
principal focus. The distance from here to the
centre of the lens is the focal length. A concave lens
spreads out light rays so that they appear to come
from a principal focus behind the lens. The focal
length is the distance from here to the lens' centre.

VIRTUAL IMAGE

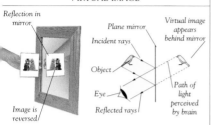

Reflection in mirror

Image is reversed

Plane mirror

Incident rays

Object

Eye

Reflected rays

Virtual image appears behind mirror

Path of light perceived by brain

When you see an object in a mirror, light rays from the object reflect from the mirror's surface into your eyes. Your brain assumes that the rays have reached your eyes by travelling in a straight line, so you see a "virtual" image that appears to be behind the mirror.

LAW OF REFLECTION

Angle of incidence   *Angle of reflection*

Light ray

Plane mirror

According to the Law of Reflection, the angle at which a light ray is reflected from a surface (the angle of reflection) is equal to the angle at which the light ray strikes the surface (the angle of incidence).

REAL IMAGES

Convex lenses and concave mirrors can focus light to form an inverted "real" image on a surface. In a movie projector, light shines through an inverted film. This is so that the image projected onto the screen appears the right way up.

CONVEX AND CONCAVE MIRRORS

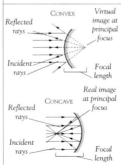

CONVEX

Reflected rays

Incident rays

Virtual image at principal focus

Focal length

CONCAVE

Reflected rays

Incident rays

Real image at principal focus

Focal length

When parallel light rays strike an outwardly curving convex mirror, they spread out as they are reflected. The rays appear to the brain to come from a principal focus behind the mirror. Parallel rays striking an inwardly curving concave mirror will reflect so that they converge at a principal focus in front of the mirror.

VISIBLE SPECTRUM

LIGHT IS WAVES of electromagnetic radiation. "White light" is a mixture of many different colours of light, each with its own frequency and wavelength. These colours make up the visible spectrum. Our eyes and brains detect colours by recognizing the different wavelengths of visible light.

SPLITTING LIGHT

A beam of white light is refracted (bent) as it enters and leaves a prism. The prism refracts different wavelengths of light by different amounts, splitting the beam of white light into the visible spectrum.

LIGHT, COLOUR, AND HEAT

The atoms of a hot object give out infrared radiation and some red light. As the object gets hotter, its atoms give out shorter and shorter wavelengths and it appears orange and then yellow. Very hot objects give out the whole spectrum and appear white.

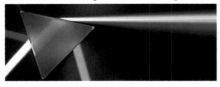

Atoms emit light at red end of spectrum

Hotter atoms emit orange light

Heated further, atoms emit yellow light

The hottest atoms now emit white light

DIFFRACTION COLOURS
All forms of wave energy "diffract", or spread out, when they pass through gaps or around objects. A diffraction grating is a glass slide engraved with narrow slits. Light rays diffract as they pass through the slits, and interference between the bent rays produces streaks of different colours.

SKY COLOUR

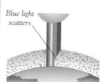

Blue light scatters

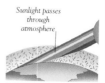

Sunlight passes through atmosphere

BLUE SKIES
The Sun gives off pure white light which is scattered by air molecules as it enters the Earth's atmosphere. Blue light is scattered more than other colours, making the sky appear blue.

RED SKIES
When the setting Sun is low in the sky, light from the blue end of the spectrum is scattered. The Sun appears orange-red because colours from this end of the spectrum pass through to our eyes but blue colours are lost.

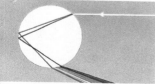

PRIMARY RAINBOW
A rainbow is visible during heavy rain, when the Sun is behind you. As rays of sunlight pass through raindrops in the sky, the raindrops act like tiny prisms. The white light is split into a spectrum inside the raindrops and reflected back as an arc of colours.

COLOUR WAVELENGTHS AND FREQUENCIES

The wavelengths and frequencies of the different colours vary according to the energy they carry. For example, red light has less energy than violet light.

COLOUR	WAVELENGTH (M)	FREQUENCY (Hz)
Violet	3.9–4.5×10^{-7}	6.7–7.7×10^{14}
Blue	4.5–4.9×10^{-7}	6.1–6.7×10^{14}
Green	4.9–5.8×10^{-7}	5.3–6.1×10^{14}
Yellow	5.8–6.0×10^{-7}	5.1–5.3×10^{14}
Orange	6.0–6.2×10^{-7}	4.8–5.1×10^{14}
Red	6.2–7.7×10^{-7}	3.9–4.8×10^{14}

Mixing colour

Paints, dyes, inks, and coloured objects get their particular colours because they absorb some light wavelengths but reflect others. This is called the subtractive process. In the additive process, colours are created by mixing different-coloured light. Each process has three pure "primary" colours, which cannot be produced by mixing other colours.

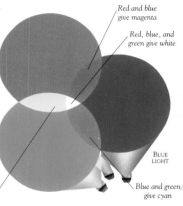

RED LIGHT

Red and blue give magenta

Red, blue, and green give white

GREEN LIGHT

Red and green give yellow

BLUE LIGHT

Blue and green give cyan

THE ADDITIVE PROCESS
Red, green, and blue are the primary additive colours. Mixing the three together gives white light. When two primary colours are mixed, the eye sees a mixture of colours that the brain interprets as a single colour, called a secondary colour. In the additive process, the secondary colours are yellow, cyan, and magenta.

In white light, shoes reflect only red light and absorb all the other colours

WHITE LIGHT

In blue light, red pigment absorbs blue light and shoes look nearly black

BLUE LIGHT

COLOUR FILTERS
A colour filter will absorb some colours but let others pass through. Placing a blue filter over a spotlight gives blue light. The filter absorbs the green and red parts of the spectrum, and allows only blue light to pass. These shoes look very different in blue light.

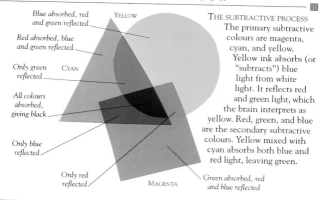

Blue absorbed, red and green reflected

YELLOW

Red absorbed, blue and green reflected

Only green reflected

CYAN

All colours absorbed, giving black

Only blue reflected

Only red reflected

MAGENTA

Green absorbed, red and blue reflected

THE SUBTRACTIVE PROCESS

The primary subtractive colours are magenta, cyan, and yellow. Yellow ink absorbs (or "subtracts") blue light from white light. It reflects red and green light, which the brain interprets as yellow. Red, green, and blue are the secondary subtractive colours. Yellow mixed with cyan absorbs both blue and red light, leaving green.

FOUR-COLOUR PRINTING

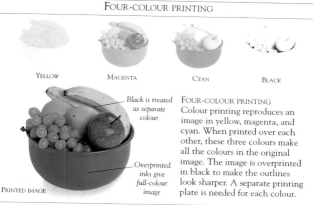

YELLOW

MAGENTA

CYAN

BLACK

Black is treated as separate colour

Overprinted inks give full-colour image

PRINTED IMAGE

FOUR-COLOUR PRINTING

Colour printing reproduces an image in yellow, magenta, and cyan. When printed over each other, these three colours make all the colours in the original image. The image is overprinted in black to make the outlines look sharper. A separate printing plate is needed for each colour.

OPTICAL INSTRUMENTS

TELESCOPES BRING distant stars into view, while microscopes enable us to examine minute objects in great detail. Optical instruments use lenses and mirrors to reveal a world that would be quite impossible to see with the naked eye alone.

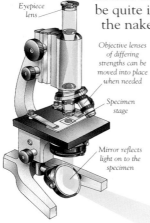

Eyepiece lens

Objective lenses of differing strengths can be moved into place when needed

Specimen stage

Mirror reflects light on to the specimen

COMPOUND MICROSCOPE
A compound microscope has more than one lens. First, it magnifies an object with a powerful "objective" lens. Then, the magnified image is enlarged by the eyepiece lens, which acts as a simple magnifying glass. The microscope may be fitted with extra lenses to give greater clarity.

TYPES OF TELESCOPE

Second mirror reflects light to eyepiece

Concave mirror

Light rays from source

Eyepiece lens magnifies image

Image

REFLECTING TELESCOPES
A reflecting telescope forms an image using a large concave mirror that gathers and concentrates light rays.

Eyepiece lens magnifies image

Light rays from source

Image

Objective lens gathers light

REFRACTING TELESCOPES
A refracting telescope uses a convex lens to refract light and form an upside-down image of a distant object.

Adjustable
eyepiece lens

BINOCULARS

A pair of binoculars consists of
two compact refracting telescopes
joined together. Each telescope
contains two prisms. The
prisms reflect light rays from
a distant object to form an
image that can be focused
with an eyepiece lens.

Prisms lengthen
distance travelled
by light rays

Prisms "fold
up" the light,
making binoculars
very compact

Viewfinder

Prism
reflects light

Light
enters lens

SLR CAMERA

In an SLR (single-lens reflex)
camera, light enters the camera
through the main lens. A mirror
reflects the light up through a prism
and out of the viewfinder. Pressing
the shutter release button raises the
mirror, so that light strikes the film
at the back of the camera.

ENDOSCOPE

Doctors look inside the body using a long
tube called an endoscope. One end of the
tube is fed into the body. Optical fibres in the
tube carry light to and from the area being
examined, which is seen with an eyepiece lens.

Mirror
Film

Doctor sees
image in
eyepiece lens

Light is internally reflected
in the optical fibres

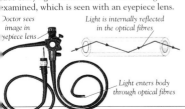

Light enters body
through optical fibres

MAGNIFICATION

A telescope with a
magnification of 100x forms
an image that is 100 times
larger than the object appears
without the telescope.
Magnification equals the
focal length of the objective
lens divided by the focal
length of the eyepiece.

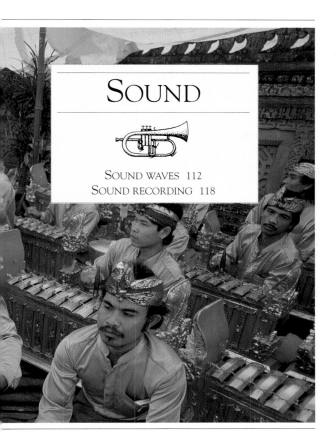

SOUND

SOUND WAVES

SOUND WAVES ARE the vibrations that occur in a
material as a sound passes through it. When we listen
to someone speak, our ears detect sound waves in the
air around us caused by the person's vibrating vocal
chords. Sound waves can travel through solids, liquids,
and gases, but not through a vacuum, because there
are no particles of matter to transmit the vibrations.

COMPOSITION OF SOUND WAVES

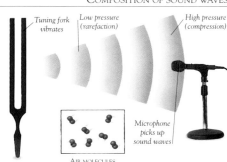

Tuning fork vibrates

Low pressure (rarefaction)

High pressure (compression)

AIR MOLECULES IN COMPRESSION

Microphone picks up sound waves

AIR MOLECULES IN RAREFACTION

Screen shows pressure changes in sound waves

COMPRESSIONS
A vibrating tuning fork causes
pressure variations in the
surrounding air. As the prongs
move outwards, they squeeze
the air, creating a high-pressure
area called a compression.

RAREFACTIONS
As the prongs move inwards
the air expands, creating a low-
pressure area called a rarefaction.
These rarefactions and
compressions travel through
air as sound waves.

Echoes bounce back from wall

Clapping sets off sound waves

HOW SONAR WORKS
A ship's sonar system emits ultrasound waves, which have a frequency above 20,000 Hz. The sound waves bounce off underwater objects. The time between sending the wave and receiving its echo reveals the depth of the object.

MAKING ECHOES
Sounds bounce off hard surfaces and return to their source as echoes. Most sounds we hear are a combination of the original sound and echoes bouncing off nearby objects.

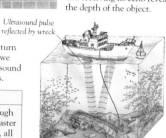

Ultrasound pulse reflected by wreck

THE SPEED OF SOUND		

Sound travels at different speeds through different materials. Sound also travels faster at higher temperatures. Unless stated, all figures are for substances at 20°C (68°F).

SUBSTANCE	SPEED M/SEC	SPEED FT/SEC
Rubber	54	177
Carbon dioxide	260	853
Air at 0°C	331	1,086
Air at 20°C	343	1,125
Air at 100°C	390	1,280
Cork	500	1,640
Water at 0°C	1,284	4,213
Hydrogen	1,286	4,219
Water at 20°C	1,483	4,865
Wood (oak)	3,850	12,631
Steel	5,060	16,601

Sound waves pile up when a jet travels at speed of sound

Shock wave released as jet breaks sound barrier

SONIC BOOM
When an aircraft breaks the sound barrier, sound waves build up in front of the aircraft. The sound forms as a massive shock wave. It is heard on the ground as a "sonic boom".

Measuring sound

The loudness of a sound depends on changes in pressure. The greater the pressure changes between the highest and lowest points of the sound wave, the louder the sound. The loudness of a sound is measured in decibels. The pitch of a sound describes how high or low a sound is. It depends on the frequency (vibrations per second) of the sound waves. The frequency of waves, including sound, light, and radio waves, is measured in hertz (Hz).

WAVEFORMS

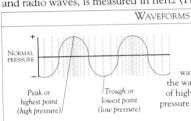

NORMAL PRESSURE

Peak or highest point (high pressure)

Trough or lowest point (low pressure)

PLOTTING SOUND WAVES
The shape of a sound wave plotted on a graph is called a waveform. The peaks and troughs of the waveform correspond to the regions of high pressure (compressions) and low pressure (rarefactions) in the sound wave.

SOFT SOUNDS
The waveform produced by a quiet sound shows little difference between the low- and high-pressure regions.

LOUD SOUNDS
As a sound gets louder, the difference between the low- and the high-pressure regions becomes much greater.

LOW-PITCHED SOUNDS
The waveform of a low-pitched sound shows few waves per second, because it has a low frequency.

HIGH-PITCHED SOUNDS
As the pitch of a sound increases, its frequency rises and the waveform shows more waves per second.

EXAMPLES ON THE DECIBEL SCALE

LOUDNESS IN DECIBELS (dB)	AMPLITUDE IN PASCALS (Pa)	POWER (INTENSITY) IN WATTS PER SQUARE METRE (W/m²)	SOUND
140	300	100	Permanent ear damage; rocket taking off 100 m (328 ft) away
120	30	1	Pain threshold; jet aircraft taking off 100 m (328 ft) away
100	3	10^{-2}	Rock concert
80	0.3	10^{-4}	Door slamming in room; busy traffic in street
60	0.03	10^{-6}	Normal conversation
30	0.0009	10^{-9}	People whispering 1 m (3.28 ft) away
10	0.00009	10^{-11}	Falling leaves 1 m (3.28 ft) away
0	0.00002	10^{-12}	Threshold of human hearing; sound just audible

ANIMAL SOUNDS

Most animals hear more frequencies of sound than they can produce. Compared with many animals, the range of sounds produced by humans is very limited. Sound below the range of human hearing is called infrasound.

BAT MAKES
10,000–120,000 Hz
HEARS
1,000–120,000 Hz

DOG MAKES
450–1,080 Hz
HEARS
15–50,000 Hz

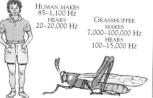

HUMAN MAKES
85–1,100 Hz
HEARS
20–20,000 Hz

GRASSHOPPER
MAKES
7,000–100,000 Hz
HEARS
100–15,000 Hz

THE DECIBEL

Loudness is measured in decibels. The decibel scale is logarithmic, meaning that a sound increase of 10 dB multiplies the intensity by 10 times. So a 20 dB increase corresponds to a sound 10 x 10 = 100 times louder.

Sound quality

If you play the same note on a piano and a guitar, the notes have different sound, because they have a different "tone", or quality. Tone depends on the way an instrument vibrates. "Pitch" is used t describe how high or low a sound is. The "acoustics" of a building refers to the way it preserves the quality of sounds made within it

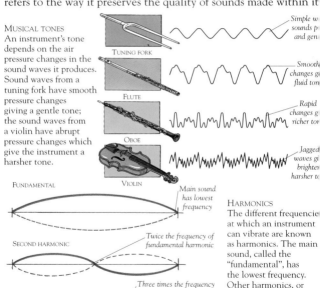

MUSICAL TONES
An instrument's tone depends on the air pressure changes in the sound waves it produces. Sound waves from a tuning fork have smooth pressure changes giving a gentle tone; the sound waves from a violin have abrupt pressure changes which give the instrument a harsher tone.

TUNING FORK

FLUTE

OBOE

VIOLIN

Simple w sounds p and gen

Smooth changes p fluid ton

Rapid changes g richer ton

Jagged waves gi brighter harsher to

FUNDAMENTAL

Main sound has lowest frequency

SECOND HARMONIC

Twice the frequency of fundamental harmonic

THIRD HARMONIC

Three times the frequency of fundamental harmonic

HARMONICS
The different frequencie at which an instrument can vibrate are known as harmonics. The main sound, called the "fundamental", has the lowest frequency. Other harmonics, or "overtones", combine with this to produce the sound you hear.

Mouthpiece *Holes*

Air column *Zero vibration (node)* *Peak of vibration (antinode)*

VIBRATIONS INSIDE A FLUTE
Blowing a flute makes the column
of air inside it vibrate. The note's
pitch depends on the length of the
column. The shorter the column,
the faster it vibrates, and the higher
the note produced. The length of
the column, and thus the pitch, is
altered by opening or closing the
holes along the flute.

Sound absorbing panel *Panel reflects sound from stage*

MUSICAL SCALES
A musical scale is a sequence of notes
that increase gradually and regularly
in pitch in a pleasing way. The note
at the bottom of the scale has
half the frequency of the
note at the top.

Reflecting panel

Building materials are carefully chosen

ARCHITECTURAL ACOUSTICS
To preserve the quality of musical sounds, concert
halls are built so that the echoes of sound waves can
be controlled. The building materials absorb just the
right amount of sound, while special sound panels inside
the hall are used to direct the sound towards listeners.

SOUND FACTS
• The science of
architectural acoustics
was founded by an
American physicist
named Wallace Sabine
(1868–1919).

• On a piano, the note
called "middle C" has a
frequency of 256 Hz.

SOUND RECORDING

ALL SOUND RECORDING systems store sound by making
copies of sound waves, either as magnetic patterns on
tape, a spiral groove on a record, or as tiny pits in a
compact disc. A recording system uses a microphone
to convert sound waves into electrical signals.

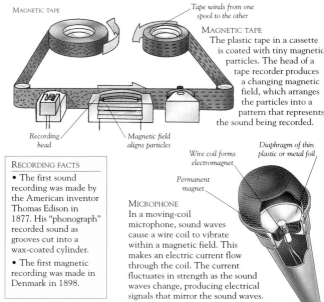

MAGNETIC TAPE

*Tape winds from one
spool to the other*

MAGNETIC TAPE
The plastic tape in a cassette
is coated with tiny magnetic
particles. The head of a
tape recorder produces
a changing magnetic
field, which arranges
the particles into a
pattern that represents
the sound being recorded.

*Recording
head*

*Magnetic field
aligns particles*

RECORDING FACTS

• The first sound
recording was made by
the American inventor
Thomas Edison in
1877. His "phonograph"
recorded sound as
grooves cut into a
wax-coated cylinder.

• The first magnetic
recording was made in
Denmark in 1898.

*Wire coil forms
electromagnet*

*Permanent
magnet*

*Diaphragm of thin
plastic or metal foil*

MICROPHONE
In a moving-coil
microphone, sound waves
cause a wire coil to vibrate
within a magnetic field. This
makes an electric current flow
through the coil. The current
fluctuates in strength as the sound
waves change, producing electrical
signals that mirror the sound waves.

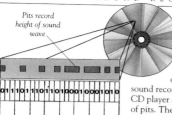

Pits record height of sound wave

COMPACT DISC

A compact disc (CD) is a plastic disc with pits pressed into its surface. The pits store sound waves as a sequence of binary numbers created by digital sound recording. As the disc spins, a laser in the CD player scans the disc and "reads" the sequence of pits. The CD player translates them into electrical pulses and feeds them to a loudspeaker.

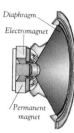

Diaphragm
Electromagnet
Permanent magnet

LOUDSPEAKER

Feeding electrical signals to a loudspeaker generates a varying magnetic field around an electromagnet. The magnet is attached to a diaphragm. The varying field causes the diaphragm to vibrate, producing sound waves.

RECORDS

Stylus *Pick-up head*

Sound can be stored as a continuous wobbling groove around a vinyl record. The stylus of a record player vibrates as it moves along the groove, setting up electrical signals in the pick-up head. The signals are then fed to loudspeakers.

SAMPLING

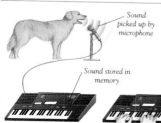

Sound picked up by microphone

Sound stored in memory

Sound played back on keyboard

A sampling system records sounds and stores them digitally. The sounds are played back through a keyboard. Pressing a key makes the system alter the pitch of a sound to match the pitch of that key. This means that the same sound can be played across a whole musical scale.

MAGNETISM
AND
ELECTRICITY

MAGNETISM

THERE IS AN invisible force exerted by magnets and electric currents called magnetism. Magnets attract iron and a few other metals, and attract or repel other magnets. Every magnet has two ends, called its north and south poles, where the forces it exerts are strongest.

MAGNETIC FORCES AT WORK

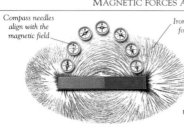

Compass needles align with the magnetic field

Iron filings show lines of force around magnet

MAGNETIC FIELD
The invisible field of force around a magnet is called a magnetic field. Here, iron filings and compasses show how the magnetic field loops around the magnet from pole to pole.

North pole   *South pole*

South pole   *South pole*

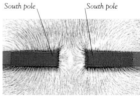

ATTRACTION
Unlike or opposite poles (a north pole and a south pole) attract each other. Iron filings scattered near the magnets reveal the lines of force running directly between the poles.

REPULSION
Like poles (two north or two south poles) repel each other. The iron filings show how the lines of magnetic force veer sharply away from each other when two like poles meet.

MAGNETIC INDUCTION

Magnetic objects contain "domains" – tiny regions of magnetism, each with two poles. The domains' poles point in all directions, so there is no overall magnetism. A magnetic field lines up the domains, magnetizing the object.

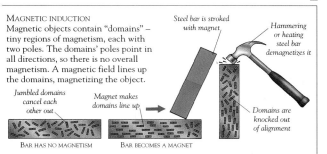

Steel bar is stroked with magnet

Hammering or heating steel bar demagnetizes it

Jumbled domains cancel each other out

Magnet makes domains line up

Domains are knocked out of alignment

BAR HAS NO MAGNETISM

BAR BECOMES A MAGNET

THE EARTH – A GIANT MAGNET

Earth's core of molten iron gives the planet its own magnetic field. The magnetic north and south poles are located near the geographic poles. The north pole of a magnet always points magnetic north.

Magnetic south is near geographic south

Earth's axis runs through geographic poles

Magnetic field is strongest near magnetic poles

MAGNETIC FACTS

• Earth's magnetic poles are at 70° N, 100° W and 68° S, 143° E, but they change constantly.

• The most magnetic substance is neodymium iron boride ($Nd_2Fe_{14}B$).

• The ancient Chinese may have made magnets by heating iron bars and letting them cool while aligned north–south.

NATURALLY MAGNETIC

Lodestone is a natural magnet. It is a form of the mineral magnetite (iron oxide). Its name means "guiding stone" and it was used in compasses 1,500 years ago.

STATIC ELECTRICITY

ELECTRICITY THAT does not flow
is static electricity. A static charge
can be produced by rubbing
a balloon against an object such
as a sweater. Electrons are
transferred from the sweater's
atoms onto the balloon's
atoms. The balloon gains a
negative electric charge and
the sweater a positive one.

BALLOON
CHARGED BY
RUBBING
(FRICTION)

*Balloon
induces
charge in
paper*

ELECTROSTATIC INDUCTION
This charged balloon can induce a
static electric charge in these pieces
of paper. The balloon's negative
charge repels electrons from the
paper's surface, giving the paper's
surface a positive charge.
Unlike charges attract, so the
balloon picks up the paper.

*Flow of
water
moves
towards
spoon*

ELECTRIC FIELD
The area in which a
charged object exerts a
force on other objects is
called an electric field.
Here, a charged plastic
spoon induces an opposite
charge in a nearby flow of
water. Force of attraction
causes the flow to bend.

*Unlike
charges
attract*

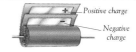

Positive charge

Negative
charge

CAPACITOR
Many electronic devices use
capacitors to build up charge and
store it until it is needed.
Inside a capacitor are two metal
plates separated by an insulator.

VAN DE GRAAFF GENERATOR

This machine generates static electricity. A charged metal comb induces a positive charge in a moving belt. When the belt reaches the metal dome, it strips electrons from the metal, giving the dome a huge positive charge.

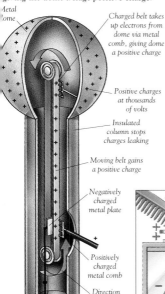

Metal dome

Charged belt takes up electrons from dome via metal comb, giving dome a positive charge

Positive charges at thousands of volts

Insulated column stops charges leaking

Moving belt gains a positive charge

Negatively charged metal plate

Positively charged metal comb

Direction of rotation of belt

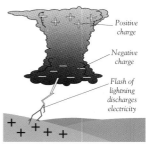

Positive charge

Negative charge

Flash of lightning discharges electricity

LIGHTNING

The tremendous build-up of static electricity inside a thundercloud induces a positive charge in the ground below. Eventually, electricity discharges from the cloud's base to the ground and back again (forked lightning), or within clouds (usually sheet lightning).

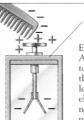

A gold-leaf electroscope detects electric charge

ELECTROSCOPE

A negatively charged comb touching the rod repels the rod's electrons to the leaves. The leaves gain electrons and each has a negative charge. The leaves push each other apart since like charges repel.

CURRENT ELECTRICITY

AN ELECTRIC CURRENT is a flow of electric charge. In a simple circuit a battery moves negatively charged electrons through metal wires. Electricity can only flow through materials called conductors. Metals are good conductors – they contain free electrons that can move easily.

INSULATED
ELECTRIC
CABLE

INSULATORS
Electrical insulators block the flow of electric current, because their atoms have no free electrons. Plastics are good insulators and are used to cover conducting wires.

Electrons stay with atoms in insulator

Free electrons in copper wire conductor

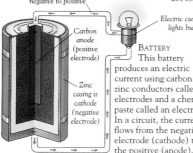

Current flows from negative to positive

Carbon anode (positive electrode)

Zinc casing is cathode (negative electrode)

Electric current lights bulb

BATTERY
This battery produces an electric current using carbon and zinc conductors called electrodes and a chemical paste called an electrolyte. In a circuit, the current flows from the negative electrode (cathode) to the positive (anode).

SI UNITS

The **ampere** or **amp** (A) is the SI unit of electric current.

The **coulomb** (C) is the SI unit of electric charge. A current of 1 amp carries a charge of 1 coulomb per second.

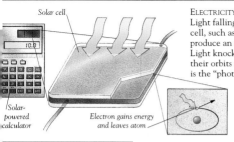

Solar cell

Solar-powered calculator

Electron gains energy and leaves atom

ELECTRICITY FROM SUNLIGHT

Light falling onto a "photovoltaic" cell, such as a solar cell, can produce an electric current. Light knocks electrons out of their orbits around atoms. This is the "photoelectric effect".

The electrons move through the cell as an electric current.

TYPES OF CURRENT

Electric current is either direct (d.c.), in which electrons flow in one direction only, or alternating (a.c.), in which electrons change direction many times each second. A battery produces d.c. current.

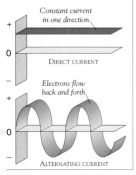

Constant current in one direction

DIRECT CURRENT

Electrons flow back and forth

ALTERNATING CURRENT

RECHARGEABLE BATTERY

A car battery can be recharged by passing an electrical current through it. This reverses the chemical changes that have occurred inside.

Dissolved metal electrodes are restored in recharging

CONDUCTIVITY OF SELECTED SUBSTANCES

Conductivities are given in units of siemens per metre (S/m): 1 S is the conductivity of a material with a resistance of 1 ohm (Ω).

SUBSTANCE	CONDUCTIVITY S/M
Copper	58,000,000
Gold	45,000,000
Tungsten	19,000,000
Graphite	70,000
Water (at 20°C)	0.0000025
Diamond	0.00000000001
Air (at sea level)	0.000000000000025

Electrical circuits

An electrical circuit is the path around which an electric current flows. A simple circuit will include a source of electrical energy, such as a battery, and conducting wires linking components, such as switches, bulbs, and resistors, that control the flow of the current.

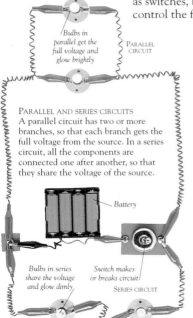

Bulbs in parallel get the full voltage and glow brightly

PARALLEL CIRCUIT

PARALLEL AND SERIES CIRCUITS
A parallel circuit has two or more branches, so that each branch gets the full voltage from the source. In a series circuit, all the components are connected one after another, so that they share the voltage of the source.

Battery

Bulbs in series share the voltage and glow dimly

Switch makes or breaks circuit

SERIES CIRCUIT

CIRCUIT SYMBOLS

—o— Switch

—|⊢ Single cell

—|⊢|⊢ Battery

—(A)— Ammeter

—(V)— Voltmeter

—⊗— Bulb

—▭— Resistor

—⊅— Variable resistor

SI UNITS
• The **volt** (V) is the SI unit of electromotive force and potential difference: 1 volt makes a current of 1 ampere produce 1 joule of energy per second.
• The **ohm** (Ω) is the SI unit of resistance: 1 ohm makes a voltage (pd) of 1 volt produce a current of 1 ampere.

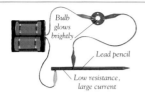

Bulb glows brightly

Lead pencil

Low resistance, large current

RESISTANCE OF A CIRCUIT
Resistance is the degree to which materials resist the flow of current. It can be used to control the flow of current through a circuit. In this circuit, the resistance of a graphite pencil lead controls current flow.

ELECTROMOTIVE FORCE
Electrons are propelled around a circuit by electromotive force (emf). The emf comes from a source of electrical energy, such as a cell or battery. Electromotive force is measured in volts.

Voltmeter

Emf of cell measures 1.5 volts on voltmeter

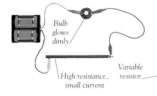

Bulb glows dimly

High resistance, small current

Variable resistor

POTENTIAL DIFFERENCE
The difference in emf between any two points in a circuit is called potential difference (pd) or voltage. Current flows because electrons always move from a point of high potential to a point of low potential.

CIRCUIT EQUATIONS
Several equations can be used to calculate the resistance (R), voltage (V), or current (I) across a conductor in an electrical circuit. These equations are:
- To calculate resistance: $R = V/I$
- To calculate voltage: $V = IR$
- To calculate current: $I = V/R$

Voltage (pd) across bulb is 2.2 volts

This "multimeter" can measure current, voltage, or resistance

ELECTROMAGNETISM

MOVING A WIRE in a magnetic field causes a current to flow through the wire. An electric current flowing through a wire generates a magnetic field around the wire. This is electromagnetism.

Electrical connection

Coils of copper wire around iron core

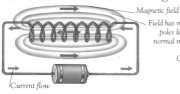

Magnetic field

Field has magnetic poles like a normal magnet

Current flow

FIELD INDUCED BY A WIRE COIL
A coil of current-carrying wire induces a stronger magnetic field than a straight wire. The coil creates a type of electromagnet called a solenoid.

POWERFUL ELECTROMAGNET
Winding a solenoid around an iron core creates a more powerful magnetic field. Here, iron filings show the strong field around this electromagnet.

GENERATORS
Electric current can be produced by rotating a wire coil between the poles of a magnet. Alternatively, a magnet may rotate while the coil remains static. Generators called dynamos give direct current, while alternators are generators that give alternating current.

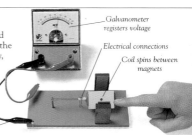

Galvanometer registers voltage

Electrical connections

Coil spins between magnets

Wires run under board

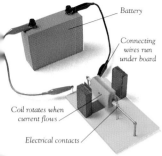

Battery

Connecting wires run under board

Coil rotates when current flows

Electrical contacts

FLEMING'S RIGHT-HAND RULE

Field

Motion

Current

FLEMING'S RULES

Fleming's rules are used to work out the directions of current, magnetic field, and motion. Fleming's right-hand rule shows the direction a current flows along a wire when the wire moves in a magnetic field (in a generator). Fleming's left-hand rule shows the direction a current-carrying wire will move in a magnetic field (in a motor).

Motion

Field

Current

FLEMING'S LEFT-HAND RULE

ELECTRIC MOTORS

In an electric motor, a current flows through a coil of wire between the poles of a magnet. The magnetic field that the coil produces interacts with the field of the magnet, forcing the coil to turn. The rotating coil can be attached to a drive shaft or flywheel to power a machine.

ELECTRIC BELL

Current induces a magnetic field in the electromagnets in this bell, pulling the hammer up to strike the gong. As the hammer moves, it breaks the circuit, then falls back to its original position.

Make-and-break circuit contact

Electromagnets

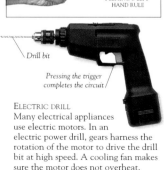

Drill bit

Pressing the trigger completes the circuit

ELECTRIC DRILL

Many electrical appliances use electric motors. In an electric power drill, gears harness the rotation of the motor to drive the drill bit at high speed. A cooling fan makes sure the motor does not overheat.

ELECTRICITY SUPPLY

ELECTRICITY PRODUCED BY generators in power stations reaches homes via a network of cables known as a grid. Resistance causes some power to be wasted as heat, and electricity is distributed at high voltage and low current to minimize this power loss.

THE ELECTRICITY GRID

PRODUCING ELECTRICITY
Power stations send electricity to substations, where "step-up" transformers increase the voltage for distribution. The power travels along underground cables or overhead lines.

CONSUMING ELECTRICITY
At "step-down" substations, the voltage is reduced by transformers to supply suitable voltages for use in industry or in the home. A local grid takes electricity to these consumers.

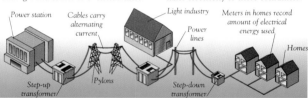

Power station

Cables carry alternating current

Light industry

Power lines

Meters in homes record amount of electrical energy used

Homes

Step-up transformer

Pylons

Step-down transformer

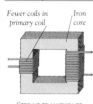

Fewer coils in primary coil

Iron core

STEP-UP TRANSFORMER

CONTROLLING VOLTAGE
Transformers consist of two wire coils wrapped around an iron core. Step-up transformers have more coils in the secondary coil and increase voltage; step-down transformers have more in the primary coil and reduce voltage.

Fewer coils in secondary coil

STEP-DOWN TRANSFORMER

CIRCUIT BREAKER

FUSE

Fuse wire melts and breaks circuit

CIRCUIT BREAKERS AND FUSES
An electrical fault may allow too much current to flow and cause wires to catch fire. Domestic circuit breakers cut off the current if it reaches dangerous levels. Fuses are the weakest link in a circuit, and burn out if the current is too strong.

TYPES OF PLUG
Electrical appliances are connected to the grid by fitting plugs into sockets. Electrical earth wires direct dangerous currents safely into the ground.

2-PIN PLUG

Earth wire

3-PIN PLUG

Fuse

3-PIN FUSED PLUG

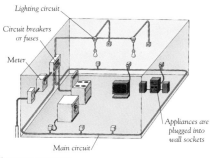

Lighting circuit

Circuit breakers or fuses

Meter

Appliances are plugged into wall sockets

Main circuit

DOMESTIC CIRCUITS
Modern houses have various circuits that supply different voltages for different purposes. For example, lighting usually takes power from a different circuit, or "ring main", to the main power circuit. Electric cookers, which use a lot of current, draw their electricity from a separate circuit.

ELECTRICITY FACTS

• In 1887, American Nikola Tesla patented an electricity supply system that transmitted alternating current.

• In homes, shops, and offices, voltage must be at 240 volts (110 volts in the USA).

ELECTRONICS

USING COMPONENTS to control electricity is known as
electronics. Integrated circuits and other electronic
components are made of semiconducting materials, such
as silicon. Adding impurities creates two types of silicon:
n-type silicon has extra, free-roaming electrons; p-type
silicon has fewer electrons,
leaving "holes".

RADIO COMPONENTS
A variable capacitor with a
coil will tune a radio into a
station. An aerial changes
radio waves into electrical
signals. Transistors amplify
the signals and a loudspeaker
converts them into sound.
The radio's volume is
controlled by a
variable resistor.

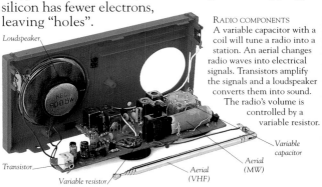

Loudspeaker

Transistor

Variable resistor

*Aerial
(VHF)*

*Aerial
(MW)*

*Variable
capacitor*

CONTROLLING CURRENT

Electronic circuits
amplify electric current,
change one-way (direct)
current to an oscillating
(alternating) current,
or switch the current
on and off.

*Transmitters are oscillators which
produce an oscillating current*

*Amplifier circuits make a
stronger copy of a weak current*

*Computer circuits use pulses of
on/off current to represent data*

SEMICONDUCTORS

Hole moves — Boron atom

Free electron moves — Arsenic atom

P-TYPE SILICON
Adding boron leaves "holes" in the silicon, since boron atoms have fewer electrons in their outer shell. The current is carried by the moving holes.

N-TYPE SILICON
Arsenic gives free electrons to the silicon, since arsenic atoms have more electrons in their outer shell. Current is carried by these free electrons.

TRANSISTOR
A transistor is a sandwich of n- and p-type silicon in a p-n-p or n-p-n arrangement. It can boost current or act as a switch. In computers, transistors switch on and off many times each second, enabling rapid calculations to be carried out.

ELECTRICAL COMPONENTS

COMPONENT	FUNCTION	SYMBOL
Capacitor	Stores charge	
Variable capacitor	Stores varying amounts of charge	
Diode	Permits current to flow in one direction only; can also be used to convert a.c. signals to d.c. signals (a "rectifier")	
Light-emitting diode (LED)	Emits light when current flows through it	
Thermistor	Converts temperature variations into current/voltage	
Aerial	Converts radio waves into a.c. signals (and vice versa)	
Microphone	Converts sound waves into a.c. current/voltage	
Loudspeaker	Converts a.c. signals into sound waves	
n-p-n transistor	Amplifies electric current, and turns it on and off	
p-n-p transistor	Amplifies electric current, and turns it on and off	

Integrated circuits

An integrated circuit is a tiny "wafer" of silicon that contains a
complete circuit with thousands of components such as transistors
and diodes. Integrated circuits, or "microchips", have made
electronic devices both smaller
and more efficient.

MANUFACTURING
The components of an
integrated circuit are made
by building up layers of
p-type and n-type
semiconductors and
other materials on a
silicon wafer. They
are linked by fine
conducting wires. A
detailed overlay plan
is made for each
layer and checked
for accuracy.

*Each plan is a
different colour*

*Tiny chip is
dwarfed by
packaging*

Transparent overlays

BINARY CODE
Microchips store data as electrical signals in
binary code. Binary numbers use only the
digits 0 and 1. The decimal number 13, for
example, is 1101 in binary form (8+4+0+1).
This converts into a binary sequence of on
(1) and off (0) electrical pulses. So 1101 is
on-on-off-on in binary code.

ENCASED CHIP
An integrated circuit is also
called a microchip. The chip is
encased in a tough plastic or
ceramic capsule, with pins that
can be soldered or plugged into a
circuit board. Many chips have
logic gates, which are patterns of
transistors that process electrical
signals. Logic gates (see right)
add up numbers in calculators.

| (ON) | (ON) | (OFF) | (ON) |
| (1x8) | (1x4) | (0x2) | (1x1) |

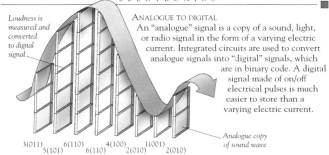

Loudness is measured and converted to digital signal

ANALOGUE TO DIGITAL

An "analogue" signal is a copy of a sound, light, or radio signal in the form of a varying electric current. Integrated circuits are used to convert analogue signals into "digital" signals, which are in binary code. A digital signal made of on/off electrical pulses is much easier to store than a varying electric current.

Analogue copy of sound wave

3(011) 6(110) 4(100) 1(001) 2(010)
  5(101) 6(110) 2(010) 2(010)

LOGIC GATES

Logic gates work with digital signals. They switch on or off depending on the type of signal they receive. "Truth tables" show what happens when signals are either applied (1) or not applied (0) to the gates.

INPUT A	INPUT B	OUTPUT
0	0	0
1	0	0
0	1	0
1	1	1

OUTPUT
A B

AND GATE
Gives an output signal when a signal is applied to one input AND to the other input.

INPUT A	INPUT B	OUTPUT
0	0	0
1	0	1
0	1	1
1	1	1

OUTPUT
A B

OR GATE
Gives an output signal when a signal is applied to one input OR to the other input, OR to both.

INPUT	OUTPUT
0	1
1	0

OUTPUT

A symbol used in designing computer circuits

INPUT

NOT GATE
The NOT gate gives an output signal when a signal is NOT applied to its input.

Weight display

MICROPROCESSOR

A microprocessor is a chip that can store instructions in an electronic memory and act on them. These scales are controlled by a single microchip. The chip converts the weight on the scales into a digital readout. It can convert the weight to or from metric or imperial units.

COMPUTERS

A COMPUTER contains thousands of electronic circuits that enable it to store and process vast amounts of information. Although a computer cannot "think" for itself, it can perform a wide variety of tasks extremely quickly. Each task is broken down into a series of simple mathematical calculations.

Monitor screen displays results

Disk drive contains software programs

Keyboard and mouse for inputting data

PERSONAL COMPUTER
The most familiar type of computer is the personal computer (PC), which can only be used by one person at a time. Most PCs consist of a keyboard and mouse, a disk drive, and a monitor screen. Machinery such as this is called "hardware".

COMPUTER PROGRAMS
A program is a set of instructions that tells a computer to carry out a specific task. The instructions may be written as "machine code" (long sets of numbers) or in a computer language such as BASIC or FORTRAN. Computer programs are called "software".

A word-processing program lets you write and edit text

SUPERCOMPUTER

Extremely powerful computers able to perform complex tasks are called supercomputers. By performing several processes at once, and by cooling their components so that they conduct electricity more efficiently, they can operate at very high speeds.

This computer is used in the study of particle physics

CRAY X-MP/48
SUPERCOMPUTER

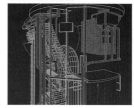

CAD BUILDING PLANS

COMPUTER-AIDED DESIGN (CAD)

Information fed into a computer "builds" an object on the screen using computer graphics. CAD allows architects and engineers to test new ideas.

VIRTUAL REALITY

A virtual-reality system enables you to interact with a computer-generated world. A headset supplies you with 3-D images, while a "data glove" lets you "touch" what you see.

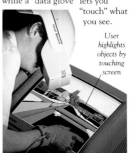

User highlights objects by touching screen

COMPUTER GENERATIONS		
GENERATION	DATE	CHARACTERISTIC
1st	1944–59	Valves (vacuum tubes)
2nd	1959–64	Transistors
3rd	1964–75	Large Scale Integrated circuits (LSIs)
4th	1975–	Very Large Scale Integrated circuits (VLSIs)
5th	Under development	"Artificial Intelligence"-based computers

Inside computers

Memory is crucial to the operation of computers because they need to be able to remember sequences of instructions in order to carry out specific tasks. In a personal computer (PC), there are two memories: read-only memory (ROM) and random-access memory (RAM), each consisting of a number of microchips.

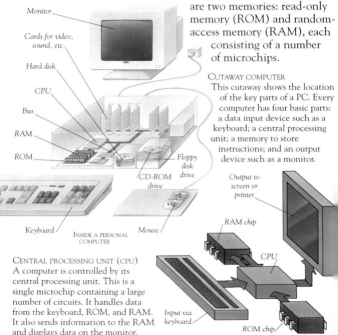

CUTAWAY COMPUTER
This cutaway shows the location of the key parts of a PC. Every computer has four basic parts: a data input device such as a keyboard; a central processing unit; a memory to store instructions; and an output device such as a monitor.

Monitor

Cards for video, sound, etc.

Hard disk

CPU

Bus

RAM

ROM

Floppy disk drive

CD-ROM drive

Keyboard

INSIDE A PERSONAL COMPUTER

Mouse

Output to screen or printer

RAM chip

CPU

Input via keyboard

ROM chip

CENTRAL PROCESSING UNIT (CPU)
A computer is controlled by its central processing unit. This is a single microchip containing a large number of circuits. It handles data from the keyboard, ROM, and RAM. It also sends information to the RAM and displays data on the monitor.

Disk coated with magnetic material

Read/write head

Track selector mechanism

HELPER BOARDS

Computers contain special circuit boards, or "cards", to carry out specific tasks needing a lot of memory. The computer passes the job on to the card, and is free to handle other tasks.

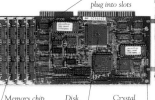

Edge connectors plug into slots

Memory chip

Disk controller

Crystal controls timing

DISKS

A hard disk stores data when a computer is off. A floppy disk is used to transfer data to other computers. The disks record data as magnetic patterns in binary code. Data is read from a disk by a disk drive.

CD-ROM

CD-ROM is a form of compact-disc player adapted for use in computers. CDs for CD-ROMs can store 450 times more information than a floppy disk, including pictures, text, sound, and video.

CD PAGE

COMPUTER TERMS	
TERM	MEANING
ROM	A computer's permanent memory, whose contents cannot be changed.
RAM	The memory used to store programs being run on the computer.
Buffer	A microchip that stores data temporarily.
Bus	A set of wires or metal strips that carries information from one part of the computer to another.
Operating system	The program that enables a computer to function.
Bit	A digit of binary information (1 or 0).
Byte	A piece of data consisting of eight bits.
Megabyte	One million bytes.
Modem	A device that allows computers to share information via a telephone network.

TELECOMMUNICATIONS

RADIO AND TELEVISION programmes – and even some
telephone conversations – are broadcast by radio
waves. The waves must first be "modulated"
(coded) so that they can carry the sound
and picture signals.

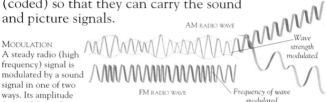

AM RADIO WAVE

*Wave
strength
modulated*

FM RADIO WAVE

*Frequency of wave
modulated*

MODULATION
A steady radio (high
frequency) signal is
modulated by a sound
signal in one of two
ways. Its amplitude
(strength) may be
modulated (AM) or its
frequency may change
(FM). The resulting
signal is transmitted
as a radio wave.

LONG-RANGE COMMUNICATIONS
Low-frequency radio waves are sent long distances by
bouncing them between the ionosphere (an ion-laden
region of the atmosphere) and the ground. High-
frequency waves pass
through the ionosphere
and are transmitted to
receiving stations on
Earth by orbiting
communications
satellites.

*High-frequency
signals are sent
via satellite*

COMMUNICATION FACTS

• In 1926, Scottish
engineer John Logie
Baird demonstrated the
first television system.

• Italian inventor
Guglielmo Marconi
made the first radio
transmission in 1894.

• US communications
satellite "Telstar" was
launched in 1962.

---

*Short waves
reflect off top
of ionosphere*

*Some radio waves
do not need to be
reflected*

*Low-frequency
waves bounce
between ionosphere
and ground*

TRANSMITTING
RADIO WAVES

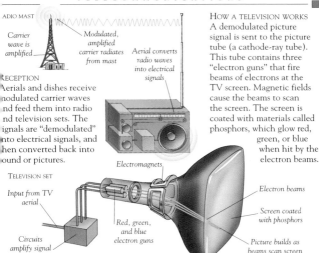

RADIO MAST

Carrier wave is amplified

Modulated, amplified carrier radiates from mast

Aerial converts radio waves into electrical signals

RECEPTION

Aerials and dishes receive modulated carrier waves and feed them into radio and television sets. The signals are "demodulated" into electrical signals, and then converted back into sound or pictures.

TELEVISION SET

Input from TV aerial

Circuits amplify signal

Electromagnets

Red, green, and blue electron guns

HOW A TELEVISION WORKS

A demodulated picture signal is sent to the picture tube (a cathode-ray tube). This tube contains three "electron guns" that fire beams of electrons at the TV screen. Magnetic fields cause the beams to scan the screen. The screen is coated with materials called phosphors, which glow red, green, or blue when hit by the electron beams.

Electron beams

Screen coated with phosphors

Picture builds as beams scan screen

TELEPHONES

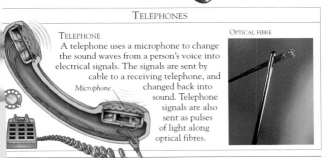

TELEPHONE

A telephone uses a microphone to change the sound waves from a person's voice into electrical signals. The signals are sent by cable to a receiving telephone, and changed back into sound. Telephone signals are also sent as pulses of light along optical fibres.

Microphone

OPTICAL FIBRE

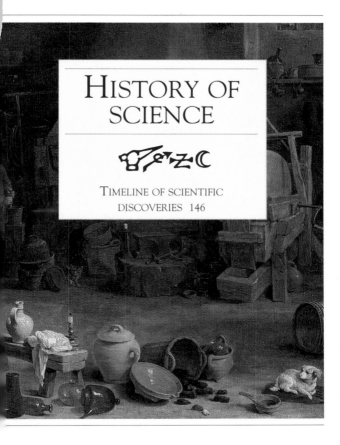

HISTORY OF
SCIENCE

TIMELINE OF SCIENTIFIC
DISCOVERIES 146

TIMELINE OF SCIENTIFIC DISCOVERIES

THIS CHART CHRONICLES some of the important discoveries in the history of science – from early ideas about the universe and the nature of force and energy to the modern world of particle physics.

c.1000 BC			AD 1650
c.1000 BC–c.260 BC	c.259 BC–AD 1599	1600–1640	1641–1650

MATTER

•c.400 BC Greek scientist Democritus suggests that matter is made out of tiny indivisible particles, which he calls atoms. •c.350 BC Aristotle, a Greek philosopher, proposes that matter is made out of four elements: earth, fire, air, and water.	•2 BC Alchemy studied in Egypt, China, and India. Alchemists try to change "base" metals such as lead into precious metals such as gold. Alchemy was the first systematic study of matter. It later reaches Europe.	•1620 A Dutch scientist called Jan van Helmont coins the word "gas". •1620s Francis Bacon, an English philosopher, develops scientific method – science based on experiment.	•1649 French philosopher Pierre Gassendi translates ancient Greek texts on the atomic theory, making the idea of the atom popular once again. •c.1650 German physicist Otto von Guericke perfects his vacuum pump.

FORCE AND ENERGY

•c.1000 BC Early civilizations rely on wind and muscle power for work and transport, and burn wood and plant matter for heat. •c.260 BC Greek scientist Archimedes discovers principle of flotation and establishes principles of mathematics.	•AD 100 Hero of Alexandria, a Greek engineer, invents the aeolipile, a forerunner of the steam turbine. It uses steam from a boiler to make a metal ball rotate.	•1600 William Gilbert, doctor to Queen Elizabeth I of England, claims that the Earth's core is like a huge magnet. •1638 Italian scientist Galileo Galilei founds mechanics (the study of force and motion). He is the first person to use a telescope.	•1643 Italian physicist Evangelista Torricelli discovers atmospheric pressure and measures it with a mercury barometer – his own invention. •1650 Blaise Pascal, a French scientist, develops his law of fluid pressures.

1651			1820
1651–1700	1701–1770	1771–1800	1801–1820

	1651–1700	1701–1770	1771–1800	1801–1820
MATTER	• 1661 Irish scientist Robert Boyle realizes the nature of elements and compounds. He suggests that the existence of small particles explains chemical reactions. • 1670 English physicist Robert Hooke develops the compound microscope.	• 1755 Scottish chemist Joseph Black identifies carbon dioxide. Also discovers latent heat. • 1766 English chemist Henry Cavendish discovers hydrogen. • 1770s French physicist and inventor Charles Coulomb studies electrostatic forces.	• 1779 French chemist Antoine Lavoisier names oxygen and shows its role in burning. Proves that air is a mixture of gases, and water a compound of oxygen and hydrogen. • 1780s Jean Antoine Chaptal, a chemist from France, sets up a factory to produce sulphuric acid.	• 1807–8 Discovery by British chemist Humphry Davy of potassium, sodium, magnesium, barium, and strontium. • 1811 Italian physicist Amedeo Avogadro formulates his law which states that equal volumes of different gases contain the same number of particles.
FORCE AND ENERGY	• 1665 English mathematician Isaac Newton formulates laws of motion and gravitation. Later discovers that light is made up of a spectrum of colours. • 1675 Danish astronomer Olë Römer measures the speed of light by observing Jupiter's moons. • 1683 French engineer John Desaguliers introduces the words "conductor" and "insulator".	• 1701 French scientist Joseph Sauveur distinguishes between sound waves and vibrations. • 1706 English scientist Francis Hawksbee develops a friction machine to generate sparks of electricity. • 1752 American scientist Benjamin Franklin proves that lightning is electrical. Also suggests that electricity consists of two types of charge. • 1765 James Watt, a Scottish engineer, builds first efficient steam engine.	• 1798 Henry Cavendish, English chemist, measures the mass of the Earth with a torsion balance. • 1799 Italian chemist Alessandro Volta devises his "voltaic pile" – the world's first battery – using different metals separated by paper discs soaked in salt solution. • 1800 André Marie Ampère, a French physicist, explores links between electric current and voltage.	• 1803 Englishman John Dalton proposes modern atomic theory – that elements and compounds are made up of atoms and molecules. • 1820 Hans Christian Oersted, a Danish physicist, discovers electromagnetism when he notices how a compass needle is deflected by a current-carrying wire.

1821			1899
1821–1840	1841–1860	1861–1880	1881–1899

	1821–1840	1841–1860	1861–1880	1881–1899
MATTER	• 1830 German chemists concentrate their studies on carbon as the basis of the "organic" chemistry of living things. • 1833 English physicist and chemist Michael Faraday discovers the laws of electrolysis.	• 1841 Swedish chemist Jöns Jacob Berzelius discovers allotropy. • 1842 French scientist Eugene-Melchor Peligot discovers uranium. • 1852 English chemist Edward Franklin introduces the concept of valency.	• 1868 Helium discovered by spectroscopic studies of the Sun. • 1869 The Russian schoolteacher Dmitri Mendeleyev classifies elements into groups by atomic weight, and devises the periodic table.	• 1896 Radioactivity discovered by French physicist Antoine Henri Becquerel. • 1897 British physicist Joseph John Thompson, discovers the electron. • 1898 Polish–French chemist Marie Curie and her French husband Pierre Curie isolate radium and polonium.
FORCE AND ENERGY	• 1831 Scientists Michael Faraday of England and Joseph Henry of the USA independently discover how to use magnetism to create electricity. • 1836 English chemist John Frederic Daniell invents the Daniell cell, the first practical and reliable source of electricity. • 1839 Englishman William Fox Talbot and Frenchman Louis Daguerre independently devise a practical photographic process.	• 1843 English scientist James Joule describes the relationship between heat, power, and work. • 1846 Laws of thermodynamics are established by William Thomson, a British scientist. • 1849 French physicist Hippolyte Fizeau makes an accurate measurement of the speed of light. • 1859 Étienne Lenoir, a Belgian engineer, invents the internal combustion engine.	• 1864 James Maxwell, a Scottish physicist, introduces the idea of the electromagnetic field. Also identifies light as a form of electromagnetic radiation. • 1876 Scottish-born inventor Alexander Graham Bell makes the first telephone. • 1879 American Thomas Edison and Englishman Joseph Swan independently produce the first electric light bulbs. Edison's is the more successful.	• 1884 Charles Parsons, an English engineer, invents the steam turbine for generating electricity. • 1888 Heinrich Hertz, a German physicist, proves the existence of radio waves. • 1888 Croatian-born physicist Nikola Tesla invents the first practical electrical induction motor. • 1894 Young Italian inventor Guglielmo Marconi makes the first radio communication.

1900			1995
1900–1911	1912–1930	1931–1945	1946–1995

MATTER

•1909 Leo Henrick Baekeland, an American chemist, produces the first stable, fully synthetic plastic – "Bakelite". •1911 The atomic nucleus is discovered by New Zealand-born physicist Ernest Rutherford. Later, he learns to convert one element into another.	•1913 Niels Bohr, a Danish physicist, discovers that electrons orbit the nucleus of an atom in shells. •1915 William Bragg and his son Lawrence Bragg invent X-ray crystallography – a way of using X-rays to explore the structure of crystals.	•1931 The neutron is discovered by James Chadwick, a British physicist. •1931 German physicist Ernst Ruska invents the electron microscope. •1939 American chemist Linus Pauling explains the nature of chemical bonds between atoms and molecules.	•1964 American physicist Murray Gell-Mann proposes the existence of quarks. •1984 Genetic fingerprinting is developed by British scientist Alec Jeffreys. •1995 Fifth state of matter, called the "superatom", is found at temperatures close to absolute zero.

FORCE AND ENERGY

•1900 Max Planck, a German physicist, proposes quantum theory – that energy is made up of small units called "quanta". From this theory, scientists deduce that light acts both as waves and as particles. •1905 German-born physicist Albert Einstein publishes his *Special Theory of Relativity*. Together with his *General Theory of Relativity* (1915), it revolutionizes the world of science and shows that mass can be converted to energy.	•1911 Dutch physicist Heike Onnes discovers superconductivity in mercury at near absolute zero. •1912 German physicist Max von Laue discovers that X-rays are electromagnetic radiation, by studying their reflection from crystals. •1912 Austrian-born American physicist Victor Hess discovers high energy cosmic radiation during high-altitude balloon flights.	•1937 First working jet engine is built by British engineer Frank Whittle. •1938 German scientist Otto Hahn and Austrian physicist Lise Meitner discover nuclear fission. •1939 German scientist Hans Bethe explains that the Sun and stars are powered by nuclear fusion. •1942 Enrico Fermi, an Italian–American physicist, builds the first nuclear reactor. •1945 The first electronic computer, ENIAC, is devised in the USA.	•1947 American physicists John Bardeen, Walter Brattain, and William Shockley invent the transistor. •1958 The first integrated circuit consisting of one piece of semiconductor is produced by US electronics engineer Jack Kilby. •1960 The laser is invented by Theodore Maiman, an American physicist. •1971 The first microprocessor, the Intel 4004, is manufactured in the USA.

UNITS OF MEASUREMENT

SCIENTISTS USE an international system of standard units, called the *Système Internationale d'Unités* (SI units). This system enables scientists in different countries to exchange the results of their experiments and calculations.

SI BASE UNITS		
The seven SI units listed here are called "base units". All other SI units are derived from them.		
QUANTITY	UNIT	SYMBOL
Mass	kilogram	kg
Length	metre	m
Time	second	s
Electric current	ampere	A
Temperature	kelvin	K
Luminous intensity	candela	cd
Amount of substance	mole	mol

SI UNITS

• The **metre** (m) is the SI unit of length; 1 metre equals the distance that light travels in 1/299,792,458 of a second through a vacuum.

• The **second** (s) is the SI unit of time: 1 second equals 9,192,631,770 vibrations of a caesium atom, as measured by an atomic clock.

CAESIUM ATOMIC CLOCK

NUMBER TERMS		
In order to describe very large and very small values, scientists use prefixes with a unit to signify multiples or fractions of a unit.		

Bottle of drink is 1×10^3 g

Jumbo jet is 4×10^8 g

PREFIX (SYMBOL)	MEANING	SCIENTIFIC NOTATION
tera (T)	× 1,000,000,000,000	10^{12}
giga (G)	× 1,000,000,000	10^9
mega (M)	× 1,000,000	10^6
kilo (k)	× 1,000	10^3
hecto (h)	× 100	10^2
deca (da)	× 10	10^1
deci (d)	÷ 10	10^{-1}
centi (c)	÷ 100	10^{-2}
milli (m)	÷ 1,000	10^{-3}
micro (µ)	÷ 1,000,000	10^{-6}
nano (n)	÷ 1,000,000,000	10^{-9}
pico (p)	÷ 1,000,000,000,000	10^{-12}

METRIC SYSTEM

Scientists use the metric system of measurement, which is based on SI units. This table gives metric units for length, area, volume, and mass, and their traditional imperial/US equivalents.

A kilogram (kg) weight is the same as 2.2 pounds (lb)

METRIC UNIT	IMPERIAL/ US EQUIVALENT
Length	
1 centimetre (cm)	0.3937 inches
1 metre (m)	3.2808 feet
1 kilometre (km)	0.6214 mile
Area	
1 square centimetre (cm²)	0.155 square inch
1 square metre (m²)	10.76 square feet
1 hectare	2.47 acres
1 square kilometre (km²)	0.3861 square mile
Volume	
1 cubic centimetre (cm³)	0.061 cubic inch
1 litre (l)	1.76 pints (imperial) 2.11 pints (US) 0.22 gallon (imperial) 0.26 gallon (US)
Mass	
1 gram (g)	0.0353 ounce
1 kilogram (kg)	2.2046 pounds
1 tonne (t)	0.9842 ton (imperial) 1.1023 tons (US)

TEMPERATURE CONVERSIONS

- To convert °C to °F, multiply by 9, divide by 5, and add 32.
- To convert °F to °C, subtract 32, divide by 9, and multiply by 5.
- To convert °C to kelvin (K), add 273.15.
- To convert kelvin (K) to °C, subtract 273.15.

BINARY SYSTEM

The standard decimal number system is based on 10. In a decimal number, each digit has ten times the value of the digit to its right. Computers use the binary system, which is based on 2. Each digit in a binary number has twice the value of the digit to its right.

BINARY				DECIMAL	
1	0	1	0	1	0
1	0	0	1		9
1	0	0	0		8
	1	1	1		7
	1	1	0		6
	1	0	1		5
	1	0	0		4
		1	1		3
		1	0		2
			1		1
			0		0

Glossary

ACID
A compound that forms hydrogen ions when it dissolves in water.

ALKALI
A base that dissolves in water.

ALLOTROPES
Different physical forms of the same element.

AMPLITUDE
The size of a vibration or the height of a wave.

ANODE
A positively charged electrode.

ATOM
The smallest part of an element that can exist.

BASE
A compound that neutralizes an acid by reacting with it to produce a salt and water.

BOILING POINT
The temperature at which a liquid becomes a gas.

CATALYST
A substance that speeds up a chemical reaction, but is left unchanged at the end of the reaction.

CATHODE
A negatively charged electrode.

CHEMICAL BONDS
The attraction between atoms, ions, or molecules.

CHEMICAL REACTION
A process in which substances combine to form new substances.

CHEMICAL SYMBOL
A letter, or letters, that represent an element.

COLLOID
A mixture of tiny particles of a substance dispersed evenly throughout another.

COMPONENT
One of two or more forces that combines to produce another force.

COMPOUND
A substance made of atoms of two or more elements joined by chemical bonds.

CONDENSATION
The change of a gas to a liquid.

CONDUCTION
The movement of heat or electricity through a substance.

CONDUCTOR
A substance through which electricity or heat flows easily.

CONVECTION
The transfer of heat through a fluid by moving currents.

CRYSTAL
A solid with a definite, geometrical shape.

DENSITY
The mass of a substance divided by its volume.

DIFFRACTION
The spreading of waves when they pass through a narrow slit.

DIFFUSION
The mixing of two or more substances by the random movement of their particles.

DISTILLATION
Separating a liquid mixture by boiling it and condensing the resulting gases.

EFFORT
A force applied to move a load.

ELECTRICAL CIRCUIT
The path around which an electric current flows.

ELECTRIC CHARGE
A quantity of electricity, produced by the loss or gain of electrons.

ELECTRIC CURRENT
A flow of electrons or ions through a substance.

ELECTRIC FIELD
The area in which an electrically charged object exerts a force on other objects.

ELECTRICITY
Energy produced by the gain, loss, or movement of electrons.

ELECTRODE
A piece of metal or carbon that collects or emits electrons in an electrical circuit.

ELECTROLYSIS
Causing a chemical change in a substance by passing an electric current through it.

ELECTROLYTE
Substance that conducts electricity when molten or in solution.

ELECTROMAGNETIC RADIATION
Energy travelling as varying electric and magnetic fields. It acts as both waves and particles of energy.

ELECTROMAGNETISM
The interaction of magnetic and electric fields.

ELECTROMOTIVE FORCE (emf)
The force that pushes electric charges round a circuit.

ELECTRON
A negatively charged particle that orbits the nucleus of an atom.

ELECTRONIC
Relating to electrical components in which electrons are conducted through a semiconductor, a vacuum, or a gas.

ELECTROSTATIC INDUCTION
The way in which an electrically charged object produces an electric charge in another object.

ELEMENT
A substance that cannot be broken down into simpler substances and that consists of only one type of atom.

ENERGY
The capacity to do work.

EQUILIBRIUM
A state of physical or chemical balance.

EVAPORATION
The change of a liquid to a gas below the boiling point, as molecules escape from the liquid's surface.

FORCE
Anything that acts to change the movement or shape of an object.

FREEZING POINT
The temperature at which a liquid changes to a solid.

FREQUENCY
The number of vibrations, or waves, passing a point, each second.

FRICTION
A force that resists motion. It is produced by surfaces or materials rubbing together.

GENERATOR
A device that converts kinetic energy into electricity.

GRAVITY
The force of attraction between any two bodies of matter.

HALF-LIFE
The time it takes for half of the atoms in a radioactive substance to decay.

Inertia
The tendency of an object to remain at rest, or to keep moving in a straight line.

Insulator
A substance that resists or blocks the flow of heat or electricity.

Integrated Circuit
A tiny chip of semiconductor that contains thousands of electronic components.

Ion
An atom that is electrically charged because it has lost or gained electrons.

Isotopes
Atoms of the same element with differing numbers of neutrons in their nuclei.

Kinetic Energy
The energy of a moving object.

Latent Heat
The heat needed for a substance to change its state without changing its temperature.

Light
The visible form of electromagnetic radiation.

Magnetic Field
The area around a magnet in which it affects other objects with its magnetism.

Magnetic Induction
The way in which a magnet produces magnetism in another object.

Magnetism
An invisible force that attracts or repels magnetic materials, and has electro-magnetic effects.

Mass
The amount of matter in an object.

Matter
Anything that occupies space and has a mass.

Melting Point
The temperature at which a solid substance becomes a liquid. It is the same as the freezing point of the substance.

Mixture
A substance made up of two or more elements or compounds that are not chemically combined.

Molecule
A group of two or more atoms linked by chemical bonds.

Momentum
The mass of an object multiplied by its velocity.

Neutron
A particle in the nucleus of an atom with no electric charge.

Nuclear Fission
A nuclear reaction in which an atom's nucleus splits into two smaller nuclei, releasing energy.

Nuclear Fusion
A nuclear reaction in which two light nuclei combine to form a single, heavier nucleus, releasing energy.

Nuclear Reaction
A change in the nucleus of an atom.

Nucleus
The dense centre of an atom, made up of protons and neutrons.

Oxidation
A chemical reaction in which a substance gains oxygen or loses hydrogen. Also a reaction in which an atom loses electrons.

pH
A measure of the acidity or alkalinity of a substance. The scale runs from 0 to 14.

PHOTON
A particle of electromagnetic radiation such as light.

PLASMA
A form of matter in which electrons are torn from their atoms because of great heat or electricity.

POTENTIAL DIFFERENCE (pd)
The difference in emf between two points in an electrical circuit.

POWER
The rate at which work is done (or energy converted from one form to another).

PRESSURE
The amount of force acting on a given area.

PROTON
A positively charged particle in the nucleus of an atom.

RADIATION
An electromagnetic wave, or a stream of particles emitted by a decaying nucleus.

RADIOACTIVITY
The decay of the nucleus of an atom, causing radiation to be given off.

RADIOISOTOPE
A radioactive form of an element.

REACTIVE
Able to take part in a chemical reaction.

REDUCTION
A chemical reaction in which a substance gains hydrogen or loses oxygen. Also a reaction in which an atom gains electrons.

REFLECTION
The way light rays bounce off a surface.

RELATIVE ATOMIC MASS
The mass of an atom compared to the mass of an atom of carbon–12.

RESISTANCE
A measure of an electrical component's opposition to the flow of electric current through it.

RESULTANT
The overall effect of two or more forces.

SALT
A compound formed by the reaction of an acid with a base. Also another name for sodium chloride.

SEMICONDUCTOR
A substance with a varying conductivity.

SOLUBILITY
A measure of how easily one substance will dissolve in another.

SOLUTION
A mixture of two substances, in which the particles of the substance are evenly mixed.

SOUND WAVE
A vibration that travels through matter.

STATIC ELECTRICITY
An electric charge held by an object, caused by the gain or loss of electrons.

SUBLIMATION
A solid changing to a gas (or vice versa) without first becoming a liquid.

UPTHRUST
The upward force on an object immersed in fluid.

VALENCY
The number of chemical bonds an atom can make with other atoms.

WAVELENGTH
The distance between the peak of one wave and the peak of the next.

WORK
Transfer of energy, or conversion of one form of energy to another.

Index

Acknowledgements

Dorling Kindersley would like to thank: Martin Wilson for design assistance and Robin Hunter for artwork; Hilary Bird for the index; Caroline Potts for picture library services; Old Royal Observatory, Greenwich; Science Museum; Natural History Museum; University of Archeology and Anthropology, Cambridge; Kodak; Peter Griffiths and Stephen Oliver for model making.

Photographers:
Philip Dowell; Colin Keates; Clive Streeter; Harry Taylor.

Illustrators:
Zirrinia Austin; Rick Blakely; Bill Botten; Peter Bull; Kyokan G Chen; Eugene Fleury; Mark Franklin; Andrew Green; Mike Grey; Nick Hall; Nick Hewetson; John Hutchinson; Stanley Cephas Johnson; Richard Lewis; Chris Lyon; Stuart Mackay; Kevin Maddison; Sergio Momo; Jim Robins; Colin Salmon; Peter Serjeant; Rodney Shackell; Guy Smith; Roger Stewart; Taurus Graphics; Raymond Turvey; Richard Ward; John Woodcock; Dan Wright.

Picture credits: t = top b = bottom c = centre l = left r = right

Bridgeman Art Library/Christie's, London, *Alchemist at Work*, David Teniers (1582-1649) 144-5. Paul Brierley 105tl. Robert Harding Picture Library/C. Aurness 32-3. The Image Bank/Hans Wolf 57cl. Kobal Collection/*Garbo Talks*, MGM/UA 103cl. Oxford Scientific Films/London Scientific Films 16br. Pictor International: 44r, 68-9, 94-5, 110-1. Science Photo Library/Alex Bartel 31tl, 43tr; James King-Holmes 139br; Patrice Loiez/CERN 21cl; Lawrence Migdale 139cl; NASA 35tr; David Nunuk 120-1; David Parker 67cr, 139tr, 143br; Royal Observatory, Edinburgh/AATB 10-11; Simon Terrey 13c; U.S. Navy 93b. Sporting Pictures (UK) Ltd. 75t. Tony Stone Images/John Lund 40tl. ZEFA: 48-9, 65cl, 91cl.

Every effort has been made to trace the copyright holders and we apologise in advance for any unintentional omissions. We would be pleased to insert the appropriate acknowledgement in any subsequent edition of this publication.